HORSES
OF THE
STORM

HORSES
OF THE
STORM

The Incredible Rescue of Katrina's Horses

KY EVAN MORTENSEN

**ECLIPSE
PRESS**

LEXINGTON, KENTUCKY

Library of Congress Control Number: 2008920356

ISBN 978-1-58150-185-8

Printed in the United States
First Edition: 2008

a division of
Blood-Horse Publications
PUBLISHERS SINCE 1916

Contents

COVER PHOTO BY BRUCE SKINNER

This book is dedicated to the thousands of volunteers and supporters who gave their time, energy, and resources to provide a place of safety and comfort to all the animals affected by hurricanes Katrina and Rita.

Louisiana Parishes

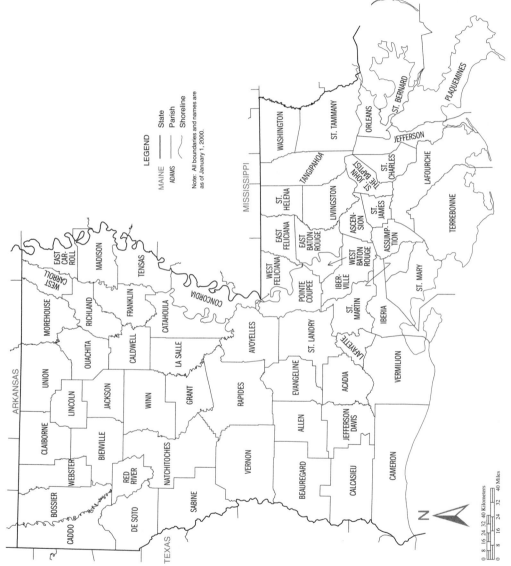

LEGEND

MAINE — State
ADAMS — Parish
〜〜 Shoreline

Note: All boundaries and names are
as of January 1, 2000.

MISSISSIPPI

ARKANSAS

TEXAS

WEST CARROLL
EAST CAR-ROLL
MADISON
TENSAS
MOREHOUSE
RICHLAND
FRANKLIN
CATAHOULA
UNION
OUACHITA
CALDWELL
LA SALLE
CONCORDIA
LINCOLN
JACKSON
WINN
GRANT
CLAIBORNE
BIENVILLE
WEBSTER
RED RIVER
NATCHITOCHES
BOSSIER
CADDO
DE SOTO
SABINE
VERNON
RAPIDES
AVOYELLES
POINTE COUPEE
WEST FELICIANA
EAST FELICIANA
EAST BATON ROUGE
WEST BATON ROUGE
IBER-VILLE
ST. LANDRY
EVANGELINE
ST. MARTIN
LAFAYETTE
ACADIA
ALLEN
JEFFERSON DAVIS
BEAUREGARD
CALCASIEU
CAMERON
VERMILION
IBERIA
ST. MARY
ASSUMP-TION
ASCEN-SION
ST. JAMES
LIVINGSTON
ST. HELENA
TANGIPAHOA
WASHINGTON
ST. TAMMANY
ST. JOHN THE BAPTIST
ST. CHARLES
ORLEANS
ST. BERNARD
JEFFERSON
LAFOURCHE
TERREBONNE
PLAQUEMINES

N

0 8 16 24 32 40 Kilometers
0 8 16 24 32 40 Miles

Timeline

8/24/2005

- Tropical Depression Katrina located south of the southern tip of Florida

8/25

- Katrina downgraded to tropical storm as it enters the Gulf of Mexico
- Louisiana State Animal Response Team (LSART) leadership meeting to organize veterinary response team

8/27 AM

- First radio and television warnings that Katrina has been upgraded to a hurricane and is potentially headed toward New Orleans

8/27 PM

- Mayor of New Orleans Ray Nagin announces voluntary evacuation of New Orleans (about 300,000 people begin evacuation)
- Eastern coastal Louisiana officials announce mandatory evacuation

8/28

- Gov. Kathleen Blanco announces mandatory evacuation of New Orleans and surrounding parishes
- National Response Plan's Emergency Support Function activated and area co-commanders report to area command center at Louisiana Department of Agriculture and Forestry (LDAF) office, Baton Rouge

8/28

- Baton Rouge, Louisiana, doubles in size as it takes in New Orleans evacuees
- Many horse owners evacuate to areas north of Lake Pontchartrain and farther away from projected Katrina path

8/29 early AM

- Hurricane Katrina makes landfall between southeast Louisiana and Mississippi coastline
- 20-plus-foot storm surge in St. Bernard and Plaquemines parishes
- An eight- to twelve-foot storm surge from Lake Pontchartrain sweeps Slidell, Louisiana, and tops levees in Orleans Parish, near Haynes Boulevard
- Wind damage and local flooding in eight other southeast Louisiana parishes (from the Pearl River area to as far west as East Baton Rouge Parish)

8/30

- Levee breaks in New Orleans cause flooding in 80 percent of Orleans Parish

8/30 PM

- Numerous calls and requests for equine rescue and response begin to come in to the LSU Veterinary Teaching Hospital and Clinic
- LSU Equine Health Studies Program (EHSP) communicates with area command (LDAF office) regarding response plans

8/31

- Establishment of the Hurricane Horse Helpline by LSU's Equine Health Studies Program to assist as a communications arm of area command center (LDAF)
- ICP (LDAF) delegates/tasks equine rescue and response operations for Hurricane Katrina-affected horses to LSU-EHSP and LSART personnel
- Press release announces the Hurricane Horse Helpline contact information
- LSART/LVMA/LSU-SVM leaders meet as a group on day two following Katrina's landfall to discuss the handling of monetary donations
- Equine shelter manager and supervising veterinarian report for duty after being appointed
- Sixty-seven horses evacuated from outer New Orleans to equine response shelter by USDA veterinary animal response teams
- Supplies gathered for care/ and feeding of sixty-seven shelter horses

9/2

- Thirty-three horses in stable condition rescued/evacuated to Katrina equine shelter

9/3

- No animal response personnel allowed access to the New Orleans area due to civil unrest and establishment of martial law

9/4

- LSART/LSU teams authorized to rescue twenty-one carriage mules and horses from downtown New Orleans

9/5

- Supplies and feed delivered and twelve horses rescued from New Orleans surrounding parishes

9/6

- Supplies and feed delivered and thirty-four horses rescued and evacuated to Katrina equine shelter

9/7

- Supplies and feed delivered and twelve horses rescued and evacuated to Katrina equine shelter

9/8

- Supplies and feed delivered and sixty-nine horses rescued and evacuated to Katrina equine shelter

9/9

- Supplies and feed delivered and seventy-nine horses rescued and evacuated to Katrina equine shelter

9/10

- Supplies and feed delivered and eleven horses rescued and evacuated to Katrina equine shelter

9/11

- Supplies and feed delivered and forty-one horses rescued and evacuated to Katrina equine shelter

9/12

- Supplies and feed delivered and one horse rescued and evacuated to Katrina equine shelter

9/13

- Supplies and feed delivered and nine horses rescued and evacuated to Katrina equine shelter

9/18

- Supplies and feed delivered and one horse rescued and evacuated to Katrina equine shelter

9/22

- Supplies and feed delivered and five horses rescued and evacuated to Katrina equine shelter

Timeline

9/24

- Category 3 Hurricane Rita makes landfall on the Texas/Louisiana border
- Rita causes severe property and livestock loss in south Louisiana
- Rita causes levee over-topping in New Orleans and additional flooding in south-central Louisiana

9/25-28

- Sixty-three horses evacuated to SugArena in New Iberia, Louisiana, in south-central Louisiana by owners and care providers
- Supplies and feed/hay delivered to SugArena

9/29

- Supplies and feed delivered and LSART/LSU rescue of seventeen horses from south-central coastal Louisiana and transported to SugArena shelter, New Iberia, Louisiana
- Five horses without food and water rescued from Orleans Parish and evacuated to Katrina equine shelter

10/1-3

- SugArena animals relocated to homes or alternative stabling

10/11

- Last group of horses (twenty) moved out of the Katrina equine shelter

(Adapted from "Equine rescue and response activities in Louisiana in the aftermath of Hurricanes Katrina and Rita, JAVMA, Vol 231, No 3. August 1, 2007." McConnico, French, Clark, Mortensen, Littlefield, and Moore)

Introduction

On Saturday evening, September 4, 2005, I sat in a small conference room in the equine veterinary hospital at Louisiana State University in Baton Rouge, Louisiana. Six days earlier, Katrina had hit the Louisiana coast. What had once been a quiet veterinary school, gently nestled against the eastern bank of the Mississippi River, had been transformed almost overnight into a full-scale emergency response unit.

News of Hurricane Katrina's wrath came pouring in with continuous updates from our small television perched high on a shelf in the corner of the large-animal reception lobby at LSU's School of Veterinary Medicine. I sat with other faculty and staff taking call after call from frantic horse owners in the southeastern regions of Louisiana pleading for help. They asked for information, for direction, for updates on flood levels, and for access into storm-affected areas. But mostly, they asked for someone to venture into Hurricane Katrina's aftermath to try to find or check on their animals. That someone was us.

We took on the task willingly, trudging through the sludge, and enduring the chaos, the contamination, the devastation, and deluge to try to locate these missing animals and provide them with shelter and care until their owners could return for them.

This is the story of how our team from LSU's School of Veterinary Medicine and countless volunteers, through a collective effort, managed to save the lives of horses and other equids, as well as dogs, cats, goats, potbellied pigs, exotic birds, wildlife, and even a few pet iguanas after a hurricane that caused more devastation and despair than any other natural disaster in the modern history of the United States.

Chapter 1

The South

With or without flooding, New Orleans is different. Before Katrina, I had been there several times and can attest that the city evokes excitement, wonder, and anticipation. Whether people have visited a hundred times or are making their maiden voyage, the Big Easy grabs them from the moment they set foot in the city limits. Beauty and history abound alongside forbidden fun. People suddenly become very accepting, and their ability to reason is altered immediately. They subconsciously decide from this point forward 3 a.m. is an acceptable bedtime.

The city combines the utmost blatant displays of wealth with poverty, greed, and humanity, not necessarily in neat striations. Two streets, one block apart: One is redolent with the scent of magnificent food, awe-inspiring architecture, and riches; the other reeks of the street-wandering homeless lying in filthy gutters. Neither tourists nor the locals seem to acknowledge much difference between the two.

The allure of this forty square miles of never-ending nightlife, open displays of sexuality, continual drunkenness, voodoo, marshland music, and unforgettable food is an autobiography of the city itself; a place continually wrapped in self conflict. It is almost as if New Orleans knows contradiction is in its nature, and like a dirt-poor child stuffing expensive candy in her mouth, it yields to desire. It possesses charms of the highest taste riddled with fascinations of the most morbid kind. One can round a corner in the French Quarter, leaving behind the flashing lights of nightclubs, nonstop karaoke, and the odorous stains of iniquity only to be caressed with a warm breeze off the Mississippi River and the smell of fresh coffee and sweet beignets at two in the morning. Whether there for a business meeting, a social occasion, or a four-day "forget life as we know it," one can't escape the magical sensation of wonder and intrigue that creeps forth from the musky swamp, clashes with the salty gulf, and brings this eerie fog we call New Orleans.

All of these thoughts and impressions came back to me as I traveled across the spillway bridge straddling Duncan Canal near the northern city limits on my first animal-rescue mission into the city on the heels of Hurricane Katrina. Catching a glimpse of the downtown skyline, I couldn't help but remember my first visit to this forbidden playground.

I had landed at New Orleans' Louis Armstrong International Airport, claimed my luggage, and stepped out into the stifling heat. It was March 2001. I hailed a cab, an old, purple Lincoln, and climbed in. The seats were worn purple leather, torn in a few places. Rubber mats protected an already-worn-out floorboard; a scrap of purple shag carpet stretched across the dashboard with little dolls scattered about, clicking against the windshield.

Judging by the driver's look, her attire, and her accent, she was probably Jamaican. She had a tassel of religious charms and beads hanging from the rearview mirror; and the entire way into the city she spoke to herself in hushed tones.

Out my tinted window I noticed the graveyards first.

"Why are the graves above ground?" I inquired.

"Flooding," she whispered.

"Oh, does it flood?" I asked.

She looked at me in the mirror, giving me a snag-toothed grin beneath bloodshot watery eyes that peered through wild, gray-ing black locks of curly hair. She stared a long time, and I wondered when she was going to put those piercing eyes back on the road.

"Does it flood?" she quietly mimicked my question in a hissing voice.

Then she gave a long, loud snort and cackled dryly to herself. She drove on, saying nothing. I suppose it does flood, I thought, wonder what that's like.

In early spring of 2005, I came to call Louisiana my home. Having been born and raised in the southwestern mountains of Colorado, I had spent the past six years working in Thorough-bred horse racing and in the equine veterinary industries in the heart of central Kentucky's Bluegrass before being offered a position with the School of Veterinary Medicine at Louisiana State University in Baton Rouge, about an hour northwest of

New Orleans.

I wasn't a veterinarian. I was a fund-raiser, a people person, and I had been invited to join the Equine Health Studies Program at LSU's veterinary school to handle marketing, public relations, fund-raising, and outreach programs. I had worked in the horse industry for years, but this was different.

The scope of the equine industry in Louisiana has no realistic measure. The horse enthusiasts range from the polo players of the North Shore to the Cajun cowboys who gather long-eared cattle in the marshes of Vermilion Bay. The differences are startling. It was the first time I realized how truly expansive the world of the equine aficionado is. The job was different than anything else I'd ever done.

The weather and terrain also were new to me. It was hot, humid, and flat. It was swampy, and the rivers were brown and slow moving. But the people were incredibly open and friendly, and I think that made all the difference in my decision to venture southward from Kentucky to set up shop.

The hospitality of the South is real. The people are truly very open and engaging, always looking everyone—acquaintances and strangers—square in the eye and continually nodding and smiling as people pass them on the sidewalk. I have always admired and appreciated this simple trait.

Baton Rouge seemed a touch dirtier than what I had expected. Perhaps it was the oil refineries to the north, south, and west, which stood like ships on the horizon, masked in a haze of pollution and floating in an endless sea of sugar cane. Maybe it was the proximity to a monstrous muddy river, a massive brown passageway filled with weathered oily barges, leading south and growing dirtier by the nautical inch. Or perhaps it was simply the industrial feel of this heartbeat of commerce constructed of mortar and steel and surrounded by heavy swamp. The place just felt rusty.

Whether it was the stage in my life or the vagaries of fate, I had come to Louisiana for a reason, and regardless of my first impressions and the bittersweet welcoming embrace of the true South, I was there. And like an arranged marriage that I dare not let fail and for reasons I yet fully understood, for better or worse, I stayed.

Through the spring and into the sweltering Louisiana summer, I was reminded of an age-old piece of wisdom: Seek first to understand. Whether it was my knee-jerk reaction to my new surroundings or my attempts to get to know an overwhelming number of locals in the horse industry, I would be reminded time and again that if I were ever to appreciate the South for what it is and find my own place within it, I needed to shut my mouth, open my ears, toss any misguided preconceptions aside, and simply let the river do the talking.

I listened, and what I heard was quite possibly the most beautiful story of history, of nature, of cultures, and of a people that my own fumbling description can never fully portray. Louisiana is a place of incredible beauty. Its story is one of triumph and joy, and also one of great loneliness and sorrow. It is a story told through the lines on the faces of farmers, oilmen, politicians, and fishermen. It is a story of progress and one of falling behind, a story of love and giving, and also one of greed.

Nature also plays a role in Louisiana in a way I hadn't really noticed in other places. Louisiana lets residents know it's hot when it's hot. When it's cold, inside or outside, people feel it. And when the winds come and the rains drive sideways in colossal buckets from blackened skies into the heart of the bayou, people know it. And like it or not, residents eventually gain a solid firsthand understanding of Mother Nature's full capabilities. At least that's how things happened in the late summer of 2005.

Chapter 2

Rain

The ongoing summer battle between humid wet rot and blazing drought was in full swing when Hurricane Katrina slammed the gulf coast of Louisiana and Mississippi in the wee hours of August 29, 2005.

There is a lot of scrambling right before a storm of this magnitude hits. Folks swarm grocery and hardware stores for a few "must haves." Cars line up in droves at the pumps. Gridlock commandeers the interstates.

Baton Rouge was in an anxious mood. The day before the storm the sky had gone black at about 2 p.m. Fast-moving gray and white clouds whisked by in different directions, framed by a dark, ominous sky. Everyone was hustling with one eye looking up. There was very little talk on the street, just constant traffic everywhere, both into and out of the city. Nobody appeared to have any collective idea of what should be done, making it confusing to a newcomer.

Some people were taking no chances. As I walked to my truck in the Wal-Mart parking lot, my shopping cart loaded with bottled water and canned goods, I watched in amazement at the sheer quantity of vehicles clogging the roadways. I saw family station wagons and SUVs stuffed inside and out with coolers, sleeping bags, and cardboard boxes full of belongings. Bungee cords strapped down brightly colored tarps, covering whatever else couldn't be left behind and could fit on the roof of a car. Concerned parents sat at the wheels, with curious kids, noses pressed against the windows, jammed in the back seats. No doubt relatives to the north and west had received anxious calls announcing unplanned visits. Yet there many families sat, probably on a half tank of gas, in an unmoving sea of traffic that stretched through the city and more than 150 miles northward along Interstate 10 from the Gulf of Mexico and westward beyond Lafayette, Louisiana.

Two blocks down the street a sign had been mounted on top of one home's garage. "Come Drink with Katrina" was splashed in black spray paint over a whitewashed piece of plywood. Eight cars were packed into the home's front yard and driveway. Two dozen college kids stood near the doorway, toasting each passing car with large white Styrofoam cups filled with red liquid.

It's a strange thing riding out a storm, particularly these days when there is so much advance warning. We have storm watches every day during late summer throughout the South. We see warnings of hurricanes for days and follow the storms on the Internet as they build and decline, move and change course somewhere over the Caribbean and across the gulf. They have names and the storms become so familiar that we speak of each one like it's the untrustworthy neighbor down the street: We can tolerate its relative proximity, we just don't want it knocking on our front door.

But despite all of the knowledge of storms, all of the technology, and all of the advance-warning systems in place, there is little people can actually do but put as much protection or physical distance between themselves and the storm. But that's about it. They can't fight it off, and they can't change its course. They are going to lose something. It may be electricity, it may be a few days of work, it may be an entire house and everything in it, or it may be something in between, but there will be loss and inconvenience. It's a very strange time.

Right before a storm arrives, there's an eerie quiet; then the winds pick up and the rain pelts down. The sky darkens to the deepest shades of blacks and grays. The streets are empty, shutters are closed, and shops are boarded up. The trees bend and sway in the torrents of wind and rain. The only sounds above the growing maelstrom are thunder and the occasional loud crack of a snapping limb or a transformer blowing out.

In the countryside, livestock are of concern as well. The dogs are brought inside whether they are "inside" dogs or not. From the windows, farmers try to catch glimpses of the cows in the field as lightning flashes. They strain their eyes to see the barn, as if seeing it standing will make everything OK. And then they wait. The power goes out; the phone stops working. And again, they wait. They consider dashing out to the pickup and running down to check on the horses, but usually they wait. Even if one does evacuate and take refuge miles from danger, waiting is still part of the hurricane experience. Eventually, the winds die, tree limbs stop snapping, the hard-driving rain lessens to a drizzle, and the world emerges to assess the damage.

Lying in my bed in Baton Rouge, I watched out my window as the heavy winds blew the rain sideways against my house. It was about 3 a.m., Monday, August 29, 2005.

The constant lightning and strange greenish-gray pall of the storm made visibility quite good, at least for a hundred feet, and that's about all anyone needed to keep an eye on his or her immediate surroundings.

As the wind reached its height, I watched the larger trees in my yard and listened to them creak and pop. Two trees in particular looked precarious. They were old pine trees, very tall and probably too skinny, with most of their weight and mass at the top. One was in the front yard and the other in the back. When the wind grew so strong that it was painful to my ears, I dashed from the front of the house to the rear, watching those pines. If one of them fell, and I was pretty sure one would, I wanted to see the direction it came so I could run to the opposite end of the house and avoid being crushed.

The storm continued into the day, but the sky rarely changed color and only slightly increased in light. Around midmorning I opened my front door and yelled across the street to my neighbor, who was standing in his doorway, surveying the situation. The street resembled a war zone; twigs, leaves, and debris were flying around in the pelting rain. He couldn't hear me very well so he took a quick look at the sky, assessed the possibility of being felled by a crashing limb or a lightning bolt, and dashed across the street to my doorstep. Stumbling inside soaking wet, he was all smiles.

"We tried to go to the grocery last night but it was crazy," he said. "Do you have any food?"

He and his wife had been out of town, having just arrived home the evening before. I gave him two cans of stew and some crackers. We talked a few minutes, and he rushed back to the safety of his home.

Cell phone service was out. Power lines were down everywhere, and limbs and debris littered the city. When the winds finally died down and I had thoroughly examined my miraculously still-standing trees, I went to check on things at work.

As I navigated my neighborhood, trees blocked roadways, electrical lines snaked along the ground, and heavy limbs sat atop some unfortunate cars and roofs. The only other manned vehicle on the road was a truck from Entergy, the local electric company, which was already beginning the seemingly impossible task of restoring power to the city.

Driving past the university lakes of LSU, I surveyed the damage throughout campus. An American flag desperately clung to its mast. Shredded, it looked like a discarded old towel hooked on a barbed-wire fence, having danced for months in the wind and the rain. I drove on.

A few people milled around the veterinary school. Some were there on emergency call, awaiting the first wave of injured animals, which had not yet arrived. Others were there because this concrete fort in which we worked was the safest spot they could think of, and they had chosen to weather the night in their offices or in the reception lobby, their cars parked safely inside the breezeway of the concrete barn, sheltered from wind and possible hail. Realizing little could be done, I ventured home and finally went to sleep.

Baton Rouge sits directly on the eastern bank of the Mississippi River, roughly eighty miles by highway northwest of New Orleans. Two main bridges link the city to the West — an older one built alongside a railway bridge in the northern part of town and the newest addition a few miles to the south that links eastward Interstate 10 traffic to the heart of "Red Stick" and vice versa.

In 1699, Sieur d'Iberville led an exploration party of about two hundred French-Canadians up the Mississippi River. On March 17, on a bluff on the east bank, they saw a cypress pole festooned with bloody animal and fish heads, which they learned was a boundary marker between the hunting territories of two of the local Houma Indian groups. The location was henceforth known as *baton rouge*, French for "red stick."

The river is still very busy. Nature's highway has served the development of hundreds of civilizations along this vital artery that penetrates the midsection of the United States. Dozens of riverboats can be seen pushing barges heavily laden with commodities to and fro anytime of day. The main port of Baton Rouge is on the western, more industrial bank while the eastern side harbors a flotilla of riverboat casinos and the *U.S.S. Kidd* battleship, now a tourist attraction. In the background is the skyline of a moderately sized downtown, which like so many others around the nation is desperately clawing its way toward a comeback.

As it winds south, the Mississippi is bordered nearly the entire way from Baton Rouge to New Orleans by small agricultural towns, oil refineries, chemical plants, farms, and old plantations. Held in place by a mountainous levee system, the river is harnessed — for the time being — and channeled where modern man believes it should go. At one point, many years past, this was all swampland. The Houma Indians carved out their existence in this sweltering marsh, the river providing for them. And in return, they allowed it to do as it wished. Through wet seasons and dry spells, the river would flood and subside, taking what she wanted and meandering wherever gravity pulled her. But mankind's necessities and the enduring spirit of progress took control of this portion of the mighty Mississippi in the 1700s, and tremendous amounts of dirt were banked up on the sides of the river for more than 150 miles to create levees, from the Port of Baton Rouge to New Orleans.

The idea of a levee system to direct and contain a waterway is not new. The Egyptians employed this engineering method thousands of years ago along the Nile. Since that time it has been adopted along riverways throughout the world. The Dutch have been using levee systems in the Netherlands for centuries. Even the romantic Danube has portions of levee systems adorning her banks. But none other can compare with what has been accomplished along the banks of the Mississippi River. A series of levee systems spanning one thousand miles of shoreline — with one continuous levee stretching more than 350 miles from

Pine Bluff, Arkansas, southward — is a marvel of modern engineering and a work forever in progress.

Slowly pushing water, wealth, and dreams, the Mississippi River snakes toward the Gulf of Mexico. She winds east and west and continually pushes south until she reaches New Orleans at the head of the delta. From there the river extends through the coastal wetlands of Louisiana, forming North America's largest alluvial fan before plunging into the salty waters of the gulf.

There is power in the movement of water, incredible power. And while it is possible to calculate that power in foot-pounds of pressure per square inch, it is impossible to appreciate unless a person has felt it. And when that power is reversed, when the tide is inevitably changed and the force of nature comes backward, when we realize we do not command the river indefinitely, nor the lakes, nor the sea; when these tremendous waters that began as tiny snowflakes in Minnesota don't find their way to the warming currents of the Caribbean but do a complete U-turn and come right through our front door, the results are simply catastrophic.

In fairness to Mother Nature, the winds and the rains of Katrina caused minimal damage in comparison to the devastation that followed. Cities throughout Louisiana felt these winds on varying levels; we heard and watched the lightning and took shelter from the torrents of rain. And then, just as it did in Baton Rouge, in Lafayette, in Slidell, and even in New Orleans, the hurricane passed. The rain stopped. Some shingles were missing, some structures were damaged, some trees were knocked down, and the power was out and might be for a couple of days.

But this had happened before.

As the anxious pressures in our hearts and minds were slowly subsiding, unbeknownst to us they were increasing in Lake Pontchartrain just above the city of New Orleans. As we took a breath, a sigh of relief, just one, the levees in New Orleans' canal system gave way. Hell and high water became one. And we would never be the same.

Chapter *3*

Helpline

Lake Pontchartrain sits just above New Orleans, occupying the northern border of the city, and Lake Borgne sits just to the southeast. Several drainage and passageway canals extend from within the city into the lakes. As the entire city of New Orleans lies below sea level, the water levels of the lake, the river, and even these canals are all above New Orleans and are therefore bordered by levees. It was here along these seemingly harmless canals that the levees were breached. These miniscule arteries that were formed to regulate drainage, protect against flooding, and provide access to ship commerce would hold the highest responsibility in the devastation of a city they were originally constructed to protect.

All of my life I had heard that New Orleans was actually below sea level. But being there, it doesn't feel below sea level. People drive or fly into the city, catch a cab, check into a hotel, and walk the streets of New Orleans. Other than the cultural differences, it feels the same as any other city. Then one day I put that below-sea-level business to the test. I had a GPS unit in my suitcase during a business trip. It was 2003, when having a GPS became a really cool thing, and I took it with me everywhere. I placed it on the sidewalk in front of the New Orleans Convention Center and stood there in broad daylight in my business suit, waiting for the device to get its satellite signals in line and give me an accurate reading. A small crowd gathered around as I focused on the GPS and attempted to explain what I was up to. The reading came back, and I proudly announced the results of my pocket-sized marvel of modern technology. We were standing eleven feet below sea level.

The topography changes throughout the city, and, not surprisingly, the older parts of town, including the French Quarter, occupy the highest levels. Therefore, they receive the least amount of flooding. But for areas eleven feet or more below sea level, even a slow trickle will eventually put an entire house under water. A massive surge not only will submerse a home but will literally wash everything away. *Everything.*

Post Katrina, New Orleans was in absolute chaos. An hour south of my warm bed, people were drowning in their homes, rushing into their stifling hot attics to escape the rising surge, and scrambling to rooftops to make their stand against an adversary intent on consuming not only everything they owned, but their lives as well. New Orleans was in big trouble.

At home in Baton Rouge, even if people didn't have power and couldn't watch the news updates on television, the sheer number of New Orleans residents pouring into the city in the

Chapter 3

days immediately following Hurricane Katrina solidly indicated something had gone seriously wrong in the Big Easy.

Baton Rouge, a city with a population of roughly 250,000 (600,000 in the entire surrounding metropolitan area) nearly doubled overnight. Stores couldn't keep supplies on their shelves; traffic on Interstate 10 didn't move for days; and cars were running out of fuel on the roads. Maintaining adequate fuel in Baton Rouge became a monumental task. Little white trash bags concealed every gas nozzle — the universal sign for "out of order." Radio stations that had formerly announced throughout the day where fuel was the cheapest now announced where gasoline could be found ... period. Obtaining any fuel took days of searching, careful planning, and waiting, all the while watching the fuel-gauge needle drift ever farther toward empty. If a fuel truck was spotted pulling into a gas station, like ravenous wolves on their prey, cars would descend upon the place holding up traffic for miles.

Nevertheless, Baton Rouge quickly became the primary staging area for search-and-rescue operations into New Orleans. Convoys of military vehicles became commonplace throughout the city. Sports facilities were turned into human-evacuee camps, parking lots became military-base camps, and storage facilities turned into makeshift morgues. The desperation for normalcy was palpable.

The storm the world came to know as Hurricane Katrina had knocked on our doors and brought more devastation to southern Louisiana than it had ever known.

Evacuees were being shuttled across the state and the nation. Busloads of rescued individuals were being transported to already overcrowded shelters in Lafayette, Baton Rouge, and Houston, Texas.

In all of this chaos, one thing became immediately apparent to us — humans were being evacuated but animals were not. So what would happen to the animals? That was the question we sought to answer. That was the one area of the rescue effort we at the veterinary school could help with. Exactly how to go about it was the problem.

As a school of veterinary medicine full of animal doctors, supplies, and so forth, we felt the immediate urge to get involved, to do something to assist, but we had no formal disaster-recovery plan nor were we receiving orders or even guidance or empowerment from any authority. We had to go with what we knew. And the only information we had was what we heard on the news, by telephone, and by rumor. We weren't in New Orleans. We didn't know how bad it truly was. Not yet. And perhaps being an hour northwest was a bigger advantage than we realized as we weren't surrounded by the immediate devastation and despair. We had to go and find it.

The veterinary school had had power during and after Katrina. The lights were always on and the phones were always working. Even if we had gone dark, backup generators would have kept us rolling. Right after Katrina hit, a few horses that had been struck by debris came into the hospital, but nothing too far out of the ordinary.

Then the phones began to ring. People were calling the veterinary school asking for help: help finding horses, help evacuating horses, help getting needed feed and supplies. Desperate pleas for assistance jammed the lines, three and four at a time.

Dr. Rustin "Rusty" Moore, the director of the equine health studies program and chief equine surgeon at LSU, had been away on business the night of the storm. When he returned, discussions immediately ensued with countless staff and faculty members to determine how we, as a veterinary school and an equine health unit, should best respond.

Dr. Moore is a bit of a spitfire. A pillar of strength and knowledge, he is respected by those at our own university and at veterinary teaching institutions around the globe. In his forties, he looks about twenty-five. In terms of energy and enthusiasm, he might really be nineteen. His youthful face, his closely cropped blond hair, and his fit physique suggest someone fresh out of boot camp. He personifies what it means to be in charge. Every day his car is in the same front-row spot of the veterinary school's parking lot. Not because he has a reserved space, but because he is at work every morning by six.

With a mountain of "can do" and possessing a very clinical mind, he was itching to do something, but it had to be done right.

"If we're going to do this," he said, "we have to do it all the way."

While we spoke frequently of wanting to support the hurricane-relief efforts, we still weren't sure exactly what needed to be done.

The state veterinary office wasn't saying much yet, and we still had heard nary a request from any organized party or governmental sector, yet here we were with all of the tools and a list full of people begging for help. As both calls for assistance with animals and offers to help besieged us, we soon realized that no single group was taking the helm on the animal-rescue front. And because LSU had begun to house some small-animal evacuees, people were seeking our help.

The telephone continued to ring.

"Hello. You've reached the LSU Equine Hospital."

"Yes, um, hello, listen, I am from Metairie [near New Orleans], and we have two small Shetland ponies. We keep them in a small stable near our house."

"Yes?"

"Well, we didn't realize the storms were going to be this bad, and since the flooding we haven't been able to get back in to look after them. They had a couple of bales of hay and a full trough of water when we left, but it's been like three days now, and we wondered if maybe you guys or maybe if you knew of someone else in the area who might be able to check on them."

There it was, right in front of us. There were horses left in the New Orleans area. And clearly, with no one anticipating the devastation, owners were desperate to know how their animals had weathered the storm and subsequent flooding. Sometimes the calls were very emotional, lengthy, and complex. And sometimes they were as simple as the inquiry above. But there were hundreds of them, and it became evident very early that someone was going to have to venture into the New Orleans area and see whether these horses had survived.

Along with Dr. Moore, countless others, and me, Dr. Becky

McConnico, an associate professor and equine clinician, immediately joined the think tank as we went back and forth for about eighteen hours forming a plan. Dr. McConnico had experience with equine rescue. But this was a different type of rescue.

Stamina would matter the most; stamina on behalf of those animals trying to survive in a devastated city that had become a fifteen-foot-deep lake and stamina on behalf of any rescue team, which would have to face these conditions, the heat and humidity, and the relentlessness of the task at hand. This wasn't a helicopter pulling a horse from a flood-swollen river before it was swept over a waterfall.

Like anything else of substance, the plan didn't come together all at once. It began with our initial effort. We followed Dr. McConnico's suggestion to establish a formal "Horse Hurricane Helpline" that could be announced to the public and would at minimum provide some limited answers, some guidance, or perhaps even a solution, as the case may be. It was the first way we could assist without a formal emergency response system in place yet. People already had been calling, so her suggestion only made sense.

Dr. McConnico was an organizer. As a mother of two teenagers and a full-time clinician and instructor at the vet school, she fully understands the meaning of time management.

We ran telephone lines and borrowed phones from various desks and constructed a makeshift call center in our conference room. What was formerly a tranquil setting used to discuss hospital cases, clinical updates, and business plans was strewn with telephone lines duct-taped at random to the floor. A computer was set up with Internet access and quick links to Mapquest and Google Earth on the desktop. The chalkboard behind the phones held a maze of scribble, proclaiming the names and cell phone numbers of literally hundreds of contacts that had been identified over the past forty-eight hours as "necessary and important personnel."

We dedicated our time in six-hour shifts, answering the phones and organizing all data collected into various lists. Callers usually fell into one of three categories. The first and most important to us initially were those who had horses that needed evacuation. The second were those who wanted to help physically with the rescue effort. The third were those who either wanted to send supplies or money, or provide available pasture if it were needed.

Our Horse Hurricane Helpline room was packed daily with members of our team. We publicized the telephone number so those with Web site, radio, or newspaper access would know they could call us for answers. What started out as designated six-hour shifts soon turned into ten- or twelve-hour gigs. As the phone began to ring continually day and night, we simply needed as much help as possible to take calls, compile the information received, call veterinarians in the affected areas, and search online or study maps to have a better understanding of the areas where we hoped to conduct our search efforts.

Though our telephone lines were initially set up for horse owners, calls from people who needed help with small animals poured in as well.

Chapter 3

One call in particular came in about three in the afternoon of September 5. A woman desperately pleaded for help finding temporary shelter for two dogs she had rescued from the floodwaters in New Orleans that morning. She had no food or fresh water for the animals, and she couldn't find any animal-rescue agencies near her in downtown New Orleans.

From Michigan, the woman had been deployed with her rescue squad to assist with animal recovery. She had been in downtown New Orleans for three days, spending hours upon hours near the Superdome, where she said thousands of displaced cats and dogs were seeking shelter from the rising waters.

I informed her she might be able to leave the animals at John M. Parker Coliseum on the LSU campus, where an animal shelter had been set up, until their rightful owners could be found. She said her convoy was making its way to Baton Rouge in a few hours and she would bring the two dogs with her.

Throughout the day, the telephone constantly rang. We jotted down each caller's information and put it in the appropriate pile. When time permitted, which it rarely did, we logged the information into a makeshift database.

We had piles of paper strewn throughout the conference center. Handwritten names and phone numbers were scratched across blackboards around the room. Maps taped to walls and on top of blackboards had "last known locations" marked with little red arrow-shaped stickers.

The phone rang again.

"Is this Mr. Mortensen?"

"Yes, it is."

"We have a woman in the small-animal hospital with two dogs from New Orleans. She is in absolute hysterics and claims that you instructed her to bring the dogs here."

I glanced at the clock. Had it really been three hours?

"I'll be right there," I said.

I left the call center and ran down the hallway to the small-animal ward. When I arrived in the lobby, a woman dressed in combat fatigues was slumped over in a chair in the corner. A dirty, red backpack was slung over her shoulders. Her face was buried in crusted hands. She looked to be in her mid-thirties and extremely tired. I could tell from the moment I saw her that she was at the end of her rope ... at least for the day. Her dirty hands were wrapped with the leashes that held her two evacuees, and when she looked up at me, her dusty face was flooded with emotion and fatigue and her cheeks were stained with tears. She and both dogs looked as though they had been through the wringer and reeked of the floodwaters they had trudged through all day.

After a few minutes spent trying to offer her some degree of comfort, I said, "We need to take these dogs to the animal rescue at the coliseum here on campus."

"But I've already walked all this way [across campus]," she said, pleadingly. "Can't you just take them in here? They need medical attention."

"And they'll get it," I said. "We just need to take them to the right place."

I loaded her and the dogs into the front seat of my truck and drove across campus to the animal-rescue check-in point. The dogs were large, tired, and confused, but something about jumping into the cab of a truck makes any dog instantly happy. Both were of mixed breeding, one being predominantly German shepherd and the other a pit-bull cross. The dogs bounced around, jumping from the front seat into the back, slinging leashes and saliva everywhere.

When we arrived in darkness at the animal-rescue center at Parker Coliseum, the sidewalk near the front entrance was lined with tables. It looked like a cross between a picket line and a massive toy drive. A multitude of handwritten posters described the process for check-in. Everything was being handled by volunteers, some of whom had been there for days, others for only minutes. For people and animals needing help, it was a crapshoot on the level of expertise they would receive. The volunteers were there with smiles on their faces and sometimes very few answers, but they were there.

"You need to wait in this line. No, wait, I can help you over here."

"Here, fill out this sheet on the dogs' backgrounds."

"Can you come over here so we can take a picture of your dogs?"

I started in, "OK, we just want to drop these dogs off. They were rescued today from New Orleans, and we don't know who owns them."

"Oh, we can't accept these animals here."

"Why not?"

"We don't take rescued animals."

"So, where do we take the rescued animals?"

"Let me check ... OK, we can take them here ... no, wait, I

think we can only accept owner give-ups."

"OK, well, we're giving them up."

"Where did you find these dogs?"

"In New Orleans."

"Are you the original owner?"

"Original owner? No."

"OK, stand in this line over here."

"When did these dogs last receive their vaccinations?"

"I don't know."

"Are you coming back to claim these dogs?"

"No."

"How long have you owned them?"

"About ten minutes."

"Do you have any current photographs of them that you can leave with us?"

"I'm afraid not."

"Here, we can take pictures of them for you and log them in. When do you plan on coming back to retrieve them?"

The woman beside me who had initially rescued the dogs was dumbfounded. She had been through God only knows what for the past three days in the heart of the storm damage, and now she was being flooded not with contaminated water and the chaos of storm rescue but with a mass of seemingly meaningless questions from volunteers simply doing their best with what they were given.

I had been wrong about this being the correct place to bring the dogs. Parker Coliseum had been set up to take in pets dropped off by their owners, who themselves were staying in shelters or other places that would not allow pets on the premises. Rescued animals were being taken to the Lamar-Dixon Expo Center in Gonzalez, Louisiana, about twenty miles south of Baton Rouge. I worked at the veterinary school, and even I didn't know what animals were to go where. It was confusion on so many levels. But, at the time, this was the only place I knew of to bring displaced animals ... period.

When the dogs were eventually accepted and taken away, I will never forget the look in that woman's eyes. She hugged them both, kissed the tops of their heads, wished them luck, and told them she loved them. She then covered her face with her hands and wept openly, surrounded by a cacophony of hundreds of barking dogs and countless human voices trying to shout over them. It was dark, and it was late. I was tired, and she was spent. The emotional drain coupled with physical exhaustion was something I was only beginning to understand fully.

Back in the truck we drove across campus to the Pete Maravich Assembly Center, LSU's basketball arena. The road between the sports complex and Tiger Stadium had been commandeered into a full-scale rescue-deployment camp. Many volunteers were housed within the arena, and my new friend would spend the night here for the next several weeks. Daily she would trek with her crew into New Orleans, rising optimistically at three each morning and returning exhausted about eleven each night.

I will never cease to be amazed at the heart of the everyday volunteer.

Chapter 4

Down River

In the event of a hurricane, horses are a big challenge to evacuate. They aren't easily thrown into the backseat of a Volvo, and they can't be snuck into a hotel room until the maid finds out. And there are more of them than people realize — even in large metropolitan areas. Think of the mounted police and of the horses and mules pulling carriages and carts. Think about the lady in the suburbs with a miniature horse in her backyard and the countless kids in surrounding neighborhoods with backyard ponies. Think about the riding stables and racetracks. Horses are everywhere, including New Orleans and its surrounding metropolitan areas.

With nearly 200,000 horses, Louisiana is an equine enthusiast's paradise. Activities for horse owners include polo, pony clubs, reining, racing, dressage, showing, jumping, eventing, and cutting. A 2005 economic impact study commissioned by the American Horse Council ranked Louisiana fifth in the nation in terms of dollars from the horse business contributed to the gross domestic product. It's a 2.45 billion dollar national industry, quite a load for an activity largely classified as a hobby. And with a climate conducive to outdoor activities nearly year-round, it isn't any wonder horses abound in the South.

During the months prior to Katrina, and then Rita, LSU had assembled an advisory council for its equine program to help identify donors and to give guidance and insight as to how the school might improve its clinic and overall service to clients. One of the council members was Dr. Debra Deprato, a thirty-something professional from New Orleans.

Dr. Deprato and I had met months earlier and had become fast friends. She broadened my business contacts by introducing me to many people she knew. A psychiatrist, she was a great listener and a strong visionary, important traits for a council member. Dr. Deprato was also an animal lover. She frequently visited LSU's small-animal clinic with her dog Claire, an English mastiff, who was being treated there for cancer. Dr. Deprato owned two pleasure horses, a chestnut Quarter Horse and an Appaloosa, and she had been keeping them just north of New Orleans at a stable on the eastern levee of the Mississippi River, in a town called St. Rose.

She called me only a day or two after the storm and asked how she might get her horses out of the area and trailer them to Baton Rouge. Her home in New Orleans had been flooded, and her office had been shut down. Both her personal and professional lives were fraught with unknowns.

I wasn't sure at the time whether her horses were truly in dire straits or whether the week's events had worn her down and this was the one thing she could do something about. When people have their homes and businesses swept away, the sadness must be incomprehensible. But perhaps even more difficult to understand is the loss of control over their lives. Seeing that her horses got out of the New Orleans area safely was something Dr. Deprato could put her efforts into. If only to assist her in that specific regard, we wanted to help.

I met Dr. Deprato at the vet school at about five on Friday morning, September 2, five days after Katrina had struck. We drove down Interstate 10, not really knowing how far we would actually be able to go, as roadblocks and military posts had been established in and around New Orleans. We still knew very little about the current state of the area. A lot of talk had been circulating about the situation farther south, what had truly happened with the levees and where the flooding was worse. There were rumors of looting, of shootings, and of rapes in the Superdome. We both wondered whether any of the rumors were true as we drove, making small talk and watching the caravan out of New Orleans, closely inspecting each vehicle to see what clues we could garner about the situation. Most of the traffic headed out of New Orleans was either officials or evacuees, many of them in buses. Traffic going toward New Orleans was scarce, a convoy of fifteen police cars, then nothing, then an ambulance, then nothing until we hit the roadblocks. As we neared the LaPlace exit, heading west toward the Mississippi River, we encountered the first of several roadblocks, each under a different authority's jurisdiction. The National Guard handled the interstate, and the state patrol handled the state highways. When we finally made it to River Road along the Mississippi heading south into St. Rose, local police manned the final barrier. With New Orleans already under martial law, law enforcement was everywhere.

During the drive Dr. Deprato mentioned that her brother-in-law also was going to try to check on his home in New Orleans. As rumors of looting spread, many homeowners were trying to return to protect whatever was left. Dr. Deprato's brother-in-law called about 10 a.m. to let us know he had made it into the city. He had navigated his way along back roads to the Huey Long Bridge, which would take him across the Mississippi River and into New Orleans. The state police had stopped him at a roadblock there, and he told them he was going to check on his house. He said the officer in charge looked at the Hummer he was driving and said, "Well, you've certainly got the right vehicle for this ... Do you have a firearm?" He said yes and showed the officer his gun. The officer looked at the gun, glanced down the road, and simply said, "OK, good luck and be careful," and let him pass through.

That simple story made the entire situation so surreal. How often do drivers get stopped on any road in America by an officer who sizes up their vehicle, asks to see their weapon, and then bids them good day? These were different times, and they were only becoming more strange.

Dr. Deprato and I made it through the first couple of roadblocks largely because of our LSU truck. We told authorities we were with the veterinary school and were going to retrieve "possibly injured animals." It was the truth, but it had an important air that somehow required no further explanation.

Turning down a muddy road, we left the broken, partially flooded asphalt behind and eased up to the barn where Dr. Deprato's horses were stabled. The owner was there.

"I just decided to weather it out," he said.

Pointing to the fences and debris strewn throughout his property, he began to recount his tale of howling winds, power loss, driving rain, and feelings of desperation. St. Rose had turned into a ghost town. We had seen practically no one on the drive since leaving the interstate.

This once-tranquil area situated next to the levee of the river now felt barren. No longer did adults and schoolchildren come to tend their horses, take lessons, and ride through the never-ending greenery of the levee. It felt as if we had reached the end of the earth. It felt abandoned and out of sync at the same time, like being caught in a scene somewhere between *The Road Warrior* and *The Twilight Zone*. Old gas barrels littered the roadsides, while rusted tin rooftops ripped from their dwellings rested against failing fences or in the branches of wind-bent trees. For the most part, unflooded pastures became landfills of never-ending sludge.

The barn housing Dr. Deprato's horses only had minor wind damage, but she wanted her horses out, along with her tack, her buckets and hay, the feed, saddles, carts of grooming equipment, wheelbarrows, everything. Her focus could now be tied to action, and she was leaving nothing behind. Her two horses came willingly, loading into the trailer without question. We spoke little as we gathered her equipment, piled it all into the truck, and headed north. As it turned out, Dr. Deprato's horses were in great shape, considering what they had endured. They had been through some pretty severe wind and rain but hadn't been struck by any debris and had had access to clean water. We would never have known this for certain, however, were it not for our efforts to go to them and assess the situation. On the return trip home, as each mile faded behind us, I could see the worry melt from Dr. Deprato's face.

While veterinarians in southern Louisiana had already been doing reconnaissance and evacuating any stables they could reach, this was the first LSU trip to bring stranded horses to a place of safety. What was done as a simple gesture of friendship and support would become our collective mission as a veterinary school for the next four weeks. We just didn't know it yet.

Chapter **5**

Begin with the End in Mind

The further we ventured into the world of animal rescue, the more we realized our challenges: the emotional challenge of all the unknowns; the logistical challenge of staying organized under trying conditions; and the physical challenge of long hours, stifling weather, and demanding schedules.

Few examples of successfully responding to all of these challenges at once, for days and even weeks on end, can compare to the success that emerged out of complete chaos at the LSU small-animal shelter at Parker Coliseum.

I had witnessed the effort in its infancy when I took my new friend with the two dogs to the coliseum a few nights after the storm. And even though I worked at the vet school, my own role on the equine team was so different and specifically focused that it was months before I learned how the small-animal shelter only a few blocks away from our call center had fared. A few thousand animals passed through the shelter, and the dedicated service provided to them is a wonderful example of the strength of the human spirit and a lesson in harnessing the power of countless willing volunteers.

As we discussed the possible resources we could provide from the equine clinic and large-animal hospital, the state veterinarian's office had commissioned the vet school to establish an animal shelter for New Orleans evacuees who were now in temporary housing, such as hotels that wouldn't allow pets. Within a day, the state had rallied veterinary school officials, who had then taken over the old Parker Agricultural Coliseum.

In their haste to leave and ride out the storm in safer environments, many New Orleans residents had arrived in Baton Rouge prior to Katrina. When the flooding began, they came in greater numbers. They filled hotels, empty apartment complexes, rental homes, and homes on the market. Some lived with friends or with relatives. Wherever an empty couch could be had, they came. And when all available housing was filled, the state set up human shelters.

Animals aren't allowed in some apartments, they aren't welcomed in many hotels, and they are frequently frowned upon in human shelters.

These were pets that owners had brought with them to escape Katrina but could find no place for them during their stay. To give owners a safe place to keep their pets for an indefinite period, LSU became the world's largest "doggy hotel."

Expecting perhaps thousands of pets in the hurricane's fallout, the state had contacted LSU in need of a small-animal shelter. Actually, the state was in need of two small-animal shelters: one to take in rescued animals whose owners were unknown and one to house animals during their temporary displacement.

LSU's first job was to see to the latter.

It was an incredible undertaking, given that the veterinary hospital had no experience or plan for this type of situation. Nevertheless, Dr. David Senior, the head of veterinary clinical sciences at LSU's vet school, took over the effort. Approximately two thousand animals would eventually come to call LSU's Parker Coliseum home over the next several weeks. The tally on a single day at the height of its operation totaled 787 dogs, 451 cats, one pig, seven rabbits, six ferrets, one hamster, one gerbil, two mice, nine tortoises, and thirty birds. It was a makeshift zoo of the strangest proportions.

All puns aside, Dr. Senior was "just what the doctor ordered." Originally from Australia, and still packing a heavy Aussie accent despite his nearly thirty years in the United States, he was a calm and positive force in the face of absolute chaos.

Per the state veterinarian's instruction, all supplies had to be procured through the state. It seemed reasonable, and for a fleeting moment the approach seemed organized. Define a space, determine what we needed, and make it happen. The feasibility of the plan, however, was another matter entirely. It took about one day for Dr. Senior to realize the state was understandably overwhelmed, and he immediately began to acquire supplies by whatever means necessary.

Like anything thrown together in haste, setting up the animal shelter began in chaos.

"It reminded me of the *The Little Rascals* at first," one volunteer said. "It was like everyone was just bringing what they had at home ... You got a fan ... bring it in. You know, like one fan was going to make a difference."

He was right in some respects. There was a bit of scrambling at first, but when you have two hundred volunteers show up in a matter of days, two hundred fans aren't far behind.

When the number of animals escalated beyond what the shelter could accommodate, more help was needed. Volunteer groups came forward, and church organizations pitched in. Within a week Parker Coliseum had structure, protocol, and animals still arriving by the hundreds.

Located on the southeastern side of campus, the coliseum is a university landmark. LSU had begun its existence as an agricultural and mechanical school and bore that title prominently in its name in the beginning. Over the years, that portion of the title has been somewhat forgotten as we've shifted to a more urban society. Parker Coliseum's importance has shifted along with the trend. While still well-used, the facility hadn't been used to its fullest capacity since its heyday when it housed stock shows, rodeos, and equestrian events. The days when thousands regularly visited to enjoy a weekend of Grand Prix jumping or to check out the local 4-H show had long passed.

With seating to accommodate a few thousand spectators and with a dirt arena floor, the coliseum for the next month became ground zero for volunteers, LSU staff, and vets making their rounds. The facility's sheer size lent itself well to the purpose and allowed appropriate separation of species. Small- and medium-sized dogs were housed in the arena. Large dogs were placed in the barn. Rabbits, ducks, pigs, and such were placed in the barn as well. Cats were housed in the hallways under the bleachers. Aggressive animals were separated from the masses and given their own spaces.

Hundreds of small metal cages housed dogs. Sad and fearful little eyes peered out. Pink tongues flickered through cage doors at helping hands reaching out to offer comfort.

It was hot. It was stuffy. It was humid. These conditions combined with the chaos of running a facility of this magnitude without experienced help increased stress.

The animal holding areas were incredibly loud. The incessant barking from all the animals in one little place was more than anyone had anticipated. Trying to maintain focus in this environment sent human emotions over the edge by the minute. One can imagine the stress that the anxiety, heat, and constant human and animal traffic placed on the animals. Those who worked in these conditions were exhausted but could actually go outside and take breaks. The animals had no options. They had to bear with us as we struggled to provide, to understand, and to attend to their daily comfort and well-being.

During the first week the shelter's lights were always on, and animals were admitted around the clock. This willingness to push forward and the unrelenting dedication to the task actually proved to be a weakness because the animals were never left undisturbed.

Dogs became aggressive; the frequency of biting incidents reached an all-time high. People broke down. Pets reacted violently to the chaos and frequently challenged those offering caring hands.

We were learning. And it soon became apparent that the place needed a break — a big break — every day. After nearly a week of nonstop chaos, the facility adopted a new, more regimented schedule. Finally, peace found a toehold.

At 8 a.m. the lights came on and the day's activities began. As new animals were admitted, those in residence were taken for walks, fed, watered, and given medication as needed; they were groomed and their cages cleaned. At noon the lights went out and activity ceased. With the first quiet in hours, the barking slowly subsided, and animals slept. At 5 p.m. the lights came back on, and work ensued as caretakers tended to each animal under their watch. At 9 p.m. the lights went out again. The magic of nightfall set in, and the animals slept. Sleep was a precious commodity, one that had to be planned for.

And then there was the unrelenting heat. Lack of air-conditioning or even airflow was stressful for everyone. To alleviate the problem, open-wire cages replaced enclosed plastic kennels, and small fans were exchanged for large fans. But increased airflow meant increased dirt flow, so carpet was laid down on the arena floor beneath the kennels. Large fans all blowing in the same direction were also placed at intervals to move air through the cat corridor, and huge box fans were hung above every stall in the barn area. The arena was a work perpetually in progress.

In addition to the arena, the shelter reception area also could be very chaotic because so many functions were performed there. Volunteers had to be signed in and given specific duties.

They were asked not only to tend to the admission and discharge of animals, but also to establish the records of each animal and set up the paperwork for a thorough veterinary evaluation. The area also provided information to the public both by phone and in person. Then there were the constant lines of people wanting to adopt or provide foster care to the pets in the facility.

The volunteers came in droves. Call it "herding cats," "making a method out of madness," pick any phrase you like. Simply channeling the volunteers was a challenge unlike any other. Make no mistake: These were incredible people with more-than-willing hearts and hands. But with so many people coming forward every day with so many different schedules for availability, organizing and educating them for their maximum effectiveness to the shelter were nearly overwhelming challenges.

LSU's Andrea Flores was highly instrumental in helping establish the volunteer program at Parker Coliseum. The first weekend, Labor Day weekend, the place swarmed with volunteers, she recalled.

"We had more volunteers than we knew what to do with ...," she said. "It was not until that Monday that we were able to actually have some sort of organizational chart, albeit crude ... We knew that after that weekend we were going to be significantly shorthanded due to people going back to work or trying to get their lives back together."

A continual challenge was not knowing how many volunteers would show up each day, she continued. "It was difficult to recruit them, keep them, train them, and, in general, depend on them."

Chapter 5

It wasn't uncommon to bring in volunteers and train them to perform specific tasks only to find them missing minutes later. Certain specific tasks had to be carried out. While few wanted to wash cages and haul feed back and forth, everyone wanted to spend time with the animals, grooming them, walking them — basically, being with them. That was understandable, but in a situation that required "all hands on deck and at their posts," it was necessary that each post be manned, glamorous or not.

For the first ten days local veterinarians and veterinary technicians willingly manned the shelter day and night. But as their private practices filled up, dividing their time between the two venues became a strain. Luckily, help wasn't far away. Hundreds of veterinarians and veterinary technicians from throughout the nation contacted the school, and relief arrived in a never-ending caravan of support.

They came from other schools, from private practices; there were small-animal experts of every kind, willing to lend hands. They brought their own supplies and additional supplies to lend to the effort. They slept wherever they could. Classrooms in the veterinary school became dorm rooms. Shifts were assigned around the clock. Walking the halls, you might find a surgeon from New York and a technician from Virginia discussing the latest developments at the shelter as they padded down the hallways in pajamas at midday.

Supervisors were appointed, and staffs were assembled. Daily operations were established according to three key areas: distinct area supervision, front personnel at the information desk, and medical staff. With the wheels in motion, Parker Coliseum began to churn forward; and in an unprecedented human effort, thousands of pets were being cared for and attended to by the loving hands of medical practitioners and civilians from throughout North America and beyond.

The vet school's Rick Ramsey, who had vast experience in animal-holding facilities and equipment, handled most logistics issues. He came with an extensive list of nationwide contacts that could locate and ship needed resources.

"Managing things we specifically ordered was one issue, but unloading, sorting, and placing in inventory the massive quantities of unsolicited supplies took a lot of manpower that was sorely needed in other locations," Dr. Senior said. "Use of the local media to solicit supplies provided tremendous assistance in the early days of the shelter before our logistics were properly set up. However, we soon learned that requests for supplies via a Web site could result in a seemingly never-ending supply of the requested item. Such is the power of the Internet."

With the resources at hand and the support to carry out the daily toil, the shelter was functioning as well as any other in the world, perhaps even better, given the sheer outpouring of willing assistance. But how long it could continue was a question no one could answer.

"Begin with the end in mind." Solid words of advice that were immediately considered, although just when the end would arrive was difficult to determine, given the frequent changes in environment and the incredible amount of unknowns. After deliberating as a team, we developed a protocol to move animals out of the shelter. Whether placing animals back home, into a permanent shelter, or up for adoption, there had to be an exit strategy for every pet under our care.

Shelter management originally placed almost all emphasis on protecting the pet for the owner, but as time passed, the pendulum swung to making sure we were doing the best thing for the pet. After six grueling weeks, we deemed that the pets would be best served when placed with an owner in a home—any home.

Faced with the initial prediction that only 30 percent to 40 percent of owners would come back to claim their pets, plans were developed to identify distant shelters to handle excess animals and establish the necessary means of transporting them there. Teams working remote from the shelter scoured the Internet and developed a list of three prominent shelters from the largest three cities in each state. Two local certified animal control officers screened this list of approximately four hundred shelters, and all the shelters that made the cut were sent e-mails asking for their help placing animals.

Fortunately, the initial prediction had been wrong. Most owners, having been displaced, gave cell phone numbers where they could be reached. The effort to contact them was surprisingly successful, and they were able to discuss the future housing options for their pets. Although many requested extensions to the deadline, most arranged to have their pets picked up on or near the deadline of September 30, 2005.

Looking back and pondering the efforts made by so many to bring hope to animals and their owners alike, one can't help but wonder at the power of the human-animal bond and the successful role it played inspiring hundreds to come forward and willingly give their time and talents, their resources and energy. While the six-week life of the shelter was relatively short, its impact was felt throughout the community, and its effectiveness has served as a model in the years since.

Chapter 6

Horse
M.A.S.H.

While we struggled to manage the many calls coming into the vet school, the state veterinarian's office was busy handling its own nonstop stream of inquiries.

Approximately thirty-six hours after Katrina hit, the state veterinarian's office received a report that sixty-seven horses needed to be evacuated from Kenner, just west of New Orleans. The hurricane had destroyed their barn and left them with neither feed or fresh water. Area veterinarians gathered trucks and trailers, halters, and leads in preparation to evacuate the animals. Authorities advised the state veterinarian's office it would have only one opportunity to collect the horses. It was all they needed. These sixty-seven horses made up the first shipment of equine evacuees hauled north for LSU to care for. They didn't come to Baton Rouge, however. The assistant state veterinarian, Dr. Martha Littlefield, along with the president of the Louisiana Equine Council, Bonnie Clark, had arranged for temporary animal shelter at the Lamar-Dixon Exposition Center in Gonzales. Located approximately halfway between Baton Rouge and New Orleans, the facility was truly a godsend.

Mary Lee Lamar-Dixon and her husband, Bill Dixon, had built the Lamar-Dixon Expo Center only a few years earlier. Bill is a fairly well-known cutting-horse trainer in the Quarter Horse world; Mary Lee is an heiress to the Lamar Advertising fortune. With some of that money, she and Bill built the $50 million Lamar-Dixon Expo Center and later turned it over to the local parish to help economic development in the community.

The property was built to accommodate everything from horse shows and motocross racing to tractor pulls, fairs, and trade shows. Situated on approximately eighty acres, it has several indoor and outdoor arenas, a number of large cultural halls and entertainment venues, more than five hundred covered stalls, and even a small chapel. As this is Louisiana, none of the barns, arenas, or stall areas are actually enclosed. They have covered roofs that allow the outside air to circulate underneath. The grounds are pristine with paved roadways, beautiful landscaping, fountains, and iron and stone fencing. It would become home to more than three thousand cats and dogs, 382 horses, and approximately 1,200 human evacuees.

I had been to Lamar-Dixon a number of times before hurricane season arrived. It was immaculate. It still is, but during the post-Katrina days it looked like a refugee camp. Behind the gates a never-ending sea of red, blue, yellow, orange, and green tents of every size and kind littered the grounds. Camping trailers and RVs were situated wherever room could be found.

Lamar-Dixon had four key things every evacuee was desperate for: regular meals, electricity, running water, and a sense of security.

Security at the front gate gradually changed from a lone hired man in a golf cart to guards in bullet-proof riot gear with machine guns pointed at the ground, fingers just inches from the trigger.

Day 1: A wave from the guard-shack window and "Hey there, are you back from LSU to check on the horses?"

Day 4: A parish policeman rising from a folding chair, "Can I help you?"

Day 7: With a hand on my door, a Louisiana State Patrol officer, "Can I see your identification?"

Day 12: Soldiers with machine guns on each side of my truck, demanding to see my access badge and inquiring how I merited entry. A thorough search of my vehicle, both on the way in and on the way out.

Upon reflection, it seems a bit strange, but at the time, with the gradual implementation, this level of security didn't faze us.

Clark became the go-to person in terms of hands-on coordination and overseeing all horses that ultimately found their way to Lamar-Dixon. She came from a lifetime of volunteer efforts in similar situations. With animal-rescue experience following Hurricane Andrew in 1993, she was ideal for the job.

About forty-five years old, with a thin frame and weathered blonde hair, Clark became a force over the next several weeks by establishing a central housing unit for rescued horses and organizing their daily care. Although the state veterinarian had formally appointed her to serve as coordinator of all the rescued horses, her efforts were really voluntary. She wasn't paid and was pretty much left on her own to come up with equipment, food, and a decent place to spend the night. She slept in a stall for the first week or two, eventually upgrading to a small pop-up trailer, and, finally, a used RV. I don't think she went home at all the first two or three weeks. During that first week I was rummaging around for some lunch one afternoon, and I remember her saying, "I think there are some granola bars in my room." She pointed toward the end of the breezeway to an open stall with a dirt floor. Nothing but bags of horse feed and a few cases of bottled water, stacked along the metal wall, were in there, along with her sleeping bag and pillow, which were shoved in a small pile in a corner.

At the outset Clark had no supplies and not much help. But she came anyway. She had left her home north of Baton Rouge, traveled about an hour south along the congested interstate, and made her way to Lamar-Dixon in time to set up a few stalls and to be on hand when the initial shipment of horses arrived. She called the veterinary school at LSU and asked what we might be willing to spare — a few buckets, some halters, sacks of feed, and so forth.

At the same time, Dr. Denny French, the LSU field service veterinarian, was asked to drop by Lamar-Dixon to check on the horses' physical condition. When those first sixty-seven horses arrived, Clark and Dr. French only had about five buckets to work with. They filled them with water and went from horse to horse, giving each a small drink, rotating buckets among stalls. There were no shavings for bedding and no grooming supplies, only what LSU could spare from "extras" found lying around the school.

A situation like this calls for personality as much as actual skill. A solid dose of optimism and an authentic sense of humor go a long way toward neutralizing the calamity and bringing order and enthusiasm to the task. And fortunately for everyone involved, Dr. French is a bit of a character. A legend in his own right, he has treated more horses and influenced more students than most would ever dream of. The great thing about Dr. French is he doesn't even know the effect he has on people. About fifty years old and standing just over six feet with a slight limp in his left leg, Dr. French has the appearance and enthusiasm of a gangly fifteen-year-old, his face continually lit with a youthful smile. When the call came asking for help treating a few equine hurricane evacuees, he and his initial crew of five fourth-year veterinary students rolled in like a M.A.S.H. unit. They checked in each animal, gave it a number and a brief description on a patient card, and attached the card to the front of its stall.

Students in their fourth and final year of veterinary school spend most of their time doing clinical work. Having spent four years in college and most of the first three years of veterinary school in the classroom, the second half of the third year and the entire fourth year of their veterinary education are spent actually doing most of the things they have learned. Call it training, hands-on experience, or clinical education, it basically involves putting their classroom learning to the test in a supervised teaching environment so that they can develop the necessary skills to practice veterinary medicine.

A veterinarian is licensed to treat all animals, large or small: fish, bird, iguana, puppy, ferret, or snake. If Linnaeus classified it, veterinarians are expected to be able to treat it. Achieving veterinary expertise with all species would be quite rare indeed, so usually students "specialize" in an area of particular interest. They may choose among small animals (dogs and cats), farm animals (cows and sheep), exotics (birds and reptiles), or horses.

To expose students to all areas of veterinary medicine, the fourth year of clinical work is divided into "rotations." Students may spend a few weeks in a group working with horses before switching to small-animal surgery. Then it's off to radiology and then on to pharmacology. The groups are small, and the instruction is specific. Those students who found themselves on the farm animal or equine rotation after Katrina could never have imagined the experience that awaited them.

As part of his teaching duties at LSU, Dr. French was in charge of the students doing service in the field. They would ride with him each day to farms and ranches and attend to the patients under his care, primarily horses. One reason veterinary schools open their animal hospitals to the public is to provide a "real life" environment and a source of patients for their students. As LSU found out about more horses needing rescue, the students came in greater numbers to assist with the effort. Those students not doing field service or not on the equine rotation came on weekends, on holidays, on whatever day they could break away. The sheer outpouring of support and their willingness to get involved were nothing short of amazing.

Veterinary students and volunteers from several local pony clubs spent an enormous amount of time simply maintaining the herd, attending to the basic needs of the horses, and keeping the overall operation working. Many calls were made to feed companies and manufacturers of medical and grooming supplies. The donations rolled in. Truckloads of sacked feed; semi-truckloads of hay; trailers of buckets, halters, lead ropes, medicines, gauze, wraps, and much more. Within a week there was more equipment, feed, and supplies on hand than can be found in some of America's best-kept barns.

Horses were groomed daily, their stalls cleaned, their access to fresh water constant. Their diets were strictly monitored and feeding instructions were attached to the front of each stall. The students knew every horse, its personality, and its eating and drinking habits.

At the horse barns (other barns had been allocated to small animals), newly arrived supplies were stacked in a never-ending pile near Clark's pop-up trailer. The first couple of stalls in the barn also were dedicated to supplies. Medicine and grooming equipment were stacked to the top of the stall walls. Halfway down the shed row aisles were thousands of pounds of sacked feed from companies such as Purina and Nutrena. Sitting carefully on pallets, the feed lined the walls of the breezeway, divided by its intended recipient (older horses, younger horses, and so forth.). At the end of the barn were several stacks of baled hay.

Additional truckloads Clark had procured from local farmers were stacked under the main arena. Many more truckloads of hay were finding their way down America's highways destined for southern Louisiana. In a matter of days, rescuing and caring for Katrina's victims had become a national undertaking.

The scene in front of the barns rarely changed in sixty days. Empty feed bags, stall shavings, and trash filled a huge dumpster. Volunteers were everywhere: in the aisles sweeping debris, in the stalls grooming horses, out front with buckets in hand getting water both for themselves and the horses. Clark was on the phone constantly. It seemed as if everyone were always on a cell phone, though service was "iffy" at best. They called for updates from LSU, called for more volunteers, tried to contact rescuers in New Orleans, called suppliers for equipment and feed donations, and called home to loved ones. Golf carts ran among barns. Movement was everywhere. Individuals seemed to understand their given roles, and, like ants in a massive colony, they were getting done.

At noon, and sometimes later in the day, everyone would rest, collectively. Tired minds and worn bodies would cast themselves in the shade in front of the barns. A few rows of tailgating chairs thrown together in the middle of the parking lot directly in front of the barn, buckets turned upside down, and a bale or two of straw completed the "rest area." With sweating brows and sunburned bodies, the volunteers would do nothing but take it easy for the first time in hours. Boxes of Meals Ready to Eat (MREs) were ravaged and coolers drained. Hundreds of empty water bottles filled the garbage bins. The area resembled a colossal campground during a camping trip that had gone on way too long.

As the horses were brought to Lamar-Dixon, Dr. French and his slew of veterinary students awaited them like an action-starved welcoming committee. The students were up to the task. They were there day and night. I rarely saw them catch their breath. Dr. French later said he no longer considered them students but colleagues. That kind of respect isn't won without showing some pretty serious grit. These kids were tough. They practically lived at Lamar-Dixon for the next month. They worked around the clock, slept little, and lived on MREs or whatever donated food was delivered that day. They admitted each horse to what was effectively a four-hundred-horse field hospital, gave the horse temporary identification, assigned it to a stall, conducted a thorough physical examination, treated any wounds or illness, and monitored its health, diet, and exercise. There wasn't a horse brought into Lamar-Dixon that wasn't touched daily by the hand of an LSU veterinary student.

Each time a truck lumbered around the corner at Lamar-Dixon and headed to the receiving barn, people rolled out of other barns from every direction. They came to hear the stories of the day, and they came to see what they could do to help.

Chapter 7

A Handful of Halters and Hope

As the students helped hold down the fort and keep things organized, we literally still were encountering roadblocks in the field. We had been trying to get into some affected areas for more than two days since we had established our hotline on August 31, but law enforcement often blocked the way, frustrating our efforts.

We weren't aware of it at the time, and we wouldn't know for several days due to lack of communications, but Dr. Jay Addison and his business partner, Dr. Ron Giardina, already had been evacuating horses from New Orleans. Both LSU graduates, Drs. Addison and Giardina are veterinarians who live near New Orleans and work at Fair Grounds Race Course treating Thoroughbred racehorses.

In the center of New Orleans is City Park, a large, open area that boasts a successful riding stable, City Park Stables. As usual, the barns at City Park were full of horses. With the projected path of the hurricane centered on New Orleans, Drs. Addison and Giardina began working day and night, transporting all of the horses they could out of City Park to the north shore of Lake Pontchartrain. Dr. Addison keeps a home and a horse farm there, in Tickfaw, and had room to accommodate a few evacuees.

A map of Louisiana shows two fingers of land along the gulf coast at the bottom right-hand side, just below New Orleans. This is the area where the Mississippi River plunges into the Gulf of Mexico. The top finger is St. Bernard Parish; the lower, Plaquemines. Here, on August 29, 2005, Hurricane Katrina came ashore in Louisiana.

After the hurricane Drs. Addison and Giardina knew the horses in the most immediate need of help would be those in the parishes of St. Bernard and Plaquemines. They spent days in these areas gathering lost horses, dropping off feed and water, and doing whatever was needed to assist the equine hurricane victims.

Drs. Addison and Giardina had been into St. Bernard Parish shortly after the storm and understood how to get around in the area. If one road was blocked, they usually knew another way to get themselves in and the horses out. They crossed the Mississippi River on ferries, took their boats, and searched entire neighborhoods. They drove their own trucks and trailers through floodwaters, over ruined roads, around downed power lines, across makeshift bridges, and up on levees to evacuate any horses they could find. They trudged through open pastures and backstreet alleys, through mud and muck for days with nothing but a handful of halters and hope. They knew the area like we didn't and were doing a tremendous job, but we needed to be able to get in and give them some help.

From our headquarters at LSU, we eventually contacted the state patrol to get the proper documentation for access to these areas. It was a nightmare to figure out the proper channels to go through to obtain permission to enter New Orleans. We first contacted the state veterinarian's office, then the local police, and we were finally routed to the state patrol. None of them had the ultimate authority to grant access to us. But one day after we contacted the state patrol, a representative from the governor's office called our hotline with some questions about health issues concerning dairy cows. The governor's office wanted to know what to do about all of the dairy cattle that could not be milked due to power losses in stricken areas. I am not a veterinarian, but having grown up on a dairy farm, milking cows, I could answer his question. Being very straightforward, I told them, "You can bring in generators, milk the cows by hand, or you can let them all dry up."

"Well, what will we do with all the milk?" he asked.

"Whatever you want; ship it north if you can or just dump it on the ground," I replied.

"What do you mean by dry up?" he continued.

I explained the term, letting him know that if the cows go without being milked, they will no longer produce milk as their bodies naturally enter another cycle. The cattle could potentially develop mastitis, but the condition usually isn't life threatening.

Chapter 7

"So, the cows won't die if we don't milk them?" he asked.

"No, they won't die if you don't milk them; they'll be in pain for a little while, and they probably won't be very happy, and neither will the dairy farmer, but they aren't going to die."

"Oh," he said, seeming very relieved, "that's what we were trying to determine. Thanks for the information."

He was about to hang up, when I said, "Hey, while we've got you on the line ..."

By the next morning we had a letter from the governor's office granting us access into all affected areas.

With that letter in hand we headed all over New Orleans and the surrounding parishes. Veterinarians and staff scrambled to find vehicles, line up volunteers, and coordinate operations. Everyone headed out fairly quickly. Those first couple of days were dangerous as some areas were still under martial law. We heard shots fired in several neighborhoods, and while we went in with gentle hearts and cotton lead ropes in hand, most of us kept firearms in our vehicles for protection. We joked to one another that we were "packing heat," but once we got down into New Orleans, it wasn't funny anymore.

As the daily calls mounted and locations of animals were charted on maps, our rescue-mission plans took shape. We divided everything into areas, pinpointing locations where several horses seemed within range of each other. Basically our modus operandi consisted of looking at the map, identifying areas with a plethora of red arrows in close proximity, and then assigning various groups to these areas, depending on what the mission would entail. Each red arrow on the map indicated at least one horse needing evacuation.

The maps were arranged and schedules developed. For the first time in days, we had a strategy. Access had been granted, rescue locations determined, and volunteers, pickups, and horse trailers had arrived. We were ready to descend into the unknown.

Chapter 8

Combing the Wreckage

On one of my first rescue trips into the city, I rode with Dr. Shannon Gonsoulin. A youthful and wiry ex-rodeo cowboy, Dr. Gonsoulin is a veterinarian from New Iberia, Louisiana, just north of Vermilion Bay. He had responded immediately to our need for manpower and supplies and had dedicated his vehicle and countless resources and personnel from his clinic to our equine rescue effort.

I didn't know Dr. Gonsoulin before Katrina, and I liked him instantly. I think it was his license plate I noticed first. It struck me as unusual to see a four-door pickup with a Louisiana tag that says "Gandhi." When I met him, though, I immediately understood the vanity plate. As I had stood in the Lamar-Dixon parking lot in the wee morning hours, a man with a friendly face sporting round, wire-rimmed glasses had sauntered up to me. He was the spitting image of the famous spiritual leader Mahatma Gandhi, only this man was wearing Wranglers and cowboy boots. The similarities did not end there — he was calm and possessed a spirit of goodwill. With Dr. Gonsoulin I experienced my first horse rescue in New Orleans and first embraced the awful deluge and the unbearable silence.

As we headed into areas in and around New Orleans in search of lost horses, I think all of us had preconceptions that combined our collective experience of the city before Katrina and the heartbreaking images we had been seeing on television for the past week.

The area was basically deserted, and we were pretty much on our own for the next twelve hours: no bathrooms, no food, and little — if any — cell phone service. Even if we did pack a lunch, we couldn't really eat it because we were covered in filth from head to toe.

Many times, when we located horses in need of rescue, especially those in the hardest-hit sections, whether it was in a flooded back alley or in a storm-shredded stable, it seemed the horses could sense what was going on. As soon as they heard our vehicles or voices, they started whinnying. They banged around and let us know they needed help.

"They were yelling when they heard us," Dr. Gonsoulin recounted. "I mean, they were hollering when we would get close."

Entering the barns, we would step up and out of the mud and funk, as most of the stables seemed to sit a little higher than the streets, but they were clogged with trash and debris. Some of the horses had been in these stalls for eight or nine days. The stall floors were torn to shreds where the horses had been digging around trying to get a foothold during the height of the storm surge. Now every stall was simply a big mud hole containing pieces of wood and debris from the flooding. A horse could either hug the side of his stall on the very little remaining dry ground, stand on top of any debris he could find, or simply stand in the flooded mud hole. We saw them doing all three. We saw them scrambling for traction, trying to avoid the filth. We saw them standing in muddy sinkholes, exhausted. And we saw one horse, mud caked from his feet to his belly, standing in his stall on two boards that stretched across the mud, just above the existing water line.

"He was standing there like he was on skis," Dr. Gonsoulin said.

At first the horses were skittish and scared. But once we got our hands on them, they rarely gave us any problems. They would give us their heads pretty well, and most accepted the halter fairly easily. Sometimes they were even a little over-anxious to get going. I had a big paint stallion practically dive into the halter when I entered his stall. He wanted it on, and he wanted out. Stall doors were like starting gates: Once they were cracked open, the occupant was coming out. There wasn't enough muscle in the world that could have made a horse go back inside. When we led the horses outside the barns, back into the sludge, it seemed as if they understood their predicament. It didn't matter how much slop we had to go through, what kind of debris was around, or how deep it was, they knew this was help and they weren't going to argue.

Even stallions or young horses, usually unruly, rarely gave us any trouble. They knew they were getting out, and with ears forward and heads up they were ready to march just about anywhere we needed them to go.

One day Toby Wallace, one of our fourth-year vet students, who hails from Arkansas, found a big stallion caught in a fence down in the Chalmette area.

"I thought he was going to really freak out when I approached him," Wallace said.

Standing chest deep in water, the horse was entangled in a barbed-wire fence. As Wallace cautiously approached, the animal did nothing. The stallion stood still as stone as Wallace gently freed him. And then he followed Wallace up and out of the water, straight to the trailer, and loaded without missing a step.

Occasionally, we would show up and find fifteen or twenty horses that we could tell had never seen a trailer in their lives. The untold trauma they'd already faced plus the added stress of helicopters flying all around was tough on them, and some weren't in the mood to cooperate. Having lived in the back pasture with little or no exposure to travel, these horses had to be introduced to the trailers and schooled in loading, and we were the ones who had to give these frightened animals their first lessons. We occasionally had to strap ropes around their rear ends, administer sedatives, or coax them with food. We pulled all the tricks we knew to get them loaded safely. One way or another, we were going to get them out, get them loaded, and get them to safety.

The rescues took a lot of hours, a lot of miles, and a lot of effort every day. We could listen to precise descriptions of what to expect and take down verbatim directions, yet, when we arrived, the situations were usually nothing like what we had envisioned from the calls we had taken. Katrina had changed everything, and nothing could take the place of actually being there.

And a lot of times, situations popped up on their own, many involving animals other than horses. One evening we were headed back to headquarters with rescued horses when we saw a flooded house with about twenty dogs huddled together on the porch. As the trailer still had a little room left, we backed it through the water to the porch and loaded them up. We got them out. It was the only thing to do.

On another occasion we spent hours combing neighborhoods near Haynes Boulevard, looking for a particular bay horse that had been spotted the day before. We had already walked several miles when we sighted the horse behind a house completely closed off by wreckage and chainlink fencing. We had used bolt cutters to clip the fence when we noticed two dogs and then three. All were German shepherds. I hesitated. I actually love dogs, but I don't love mean dogs, and they looked mean. They saw us and slowly rose to their feet and began to walk away. One was limping. It was then I realized the toll the storm had taken. Weakened by a lack of food and clean water, these dogs were starving to death. After catching the horse and tearing enough fence away to make a hole sizeable enough to put a horse through, we looked around for the dogs again, not out of fear this time, but out of compassion and in the hopes that if we could catch them we might be able to take them back as well.

They were gone.

Minutes later we encountered a yellow Lab. Actually, he found us as we walked a muddy alley where some miniature horses were reported to have been housed. We found the minis in a small pasture behind several homes. We were in the middle of nowhere really — way back deep in some abandoned neighborhood. One miniature horse and two very skinny ponies were running wild in a pasture next to what looked to be an abandoned singlewide trailer. We stood there with our new dog, wondering how we were going to catch them. Then a little old lady emerged from the trailer. I couldn't believe it. She had a little plastic container.

"Have you come for the horses?" she asked.

We told her yes and wondered how she had survived and why she was still here. She didn't say. She just handed us the container.

"I've been giving them this every day," she added.

It was a plastic jug of Red Cell, a liquid blood-building vitamin supplement meant to provide energy and enhance a horse's appetite. That was it. That was all the horses had been eating, along with whatever bit of dead grass and weeds they could forage in the area. They looked about as vibrant as the yellow Lab that now refused to leave our side.

We caught the horses, and they had more energy than we expected, given that they had been living on a steady diet of Red Cell. An excited miniature horse at the end of a rope is a joy. It really can't be led — only accompanied and nudged along. We bid the lady good day as she refused to leave her home.

As we headed toward the truck, we found a small group of goats in a little pen behind a ruined home. Goats are good climbers, and I think that was how they had weathered the storm. When they have a really good reason, they can even climb trees that have a few good low-hanging branches. And they proved it when the yellow Lab rushed into their pen, determined to put an end to his weeklong hunger. With our hands full of miniature horses, we stopped only long enough to chase the Lab from the pen.

Having loaded the miniature horses, we returned for the goats. There must have been half a dozen of them. Some were half buried in the mud, and though still living, they lost their will to go on. The dog returned and lunged at these inert goats, but they wouldn't even stand to flee. The ones with some spirit left scampered up a bending tree trunk in the pen. I don't recall whether the tree was actually growing out of the ground or a result of the storm, but a tree, now full of goats, sat in the middle of this tiny muddy pen.

We fashioned halters out of yellow twine, and we plucked the goats one at a time from the mire, from the water, from the tree, from wherever we could get hold of them. For more than an hour we fought to keep goats from dying in the mud, to keep the yellow Lab from killing them, and to keep the whole muddy mess moving toward the truck.

Locking the goats, the bay horse, and the miniatures in the front of the trailer, we tied the dog toward the back, prayed they wouldn't get loose and kill each other, and headed north toward Lamar-Dixon.

Some days we would rescue sixty or seventy horses, other days it was only one or two, and sometimes it was none at all. One day we would find ourselves sitting in Baton Rouge answering a phone for twelve hours straight, staring at maps, and trying to coordinate the next day's rescue attempts; the next day we'd be in Orleans Parish, leading a horse with one hand and a goat with the other while wading through the flooded filth.

The days following Katrina tested our hearts, and not a soul went untouched by the experience.

Many owners weathered the storm because they would not leave their pets behind. The only way authorities could get them to leave was for our teams to transport their pets to safety. Many times, as soon as we rolled into an area, local law enforcement would bring residents to us, and we would accompany them to their homes to retrieve their pets. Once their pets were safely in our hands, then, and only then, would people agree to be evacuated.

On one particular evening, in Chalmette, LSU veterinarians Dr. Jeremy Hubert and Dr. Lee Ann Fugler were asked to check on a woman who claimed to have forty dogs that needed to be transported out of the area. With one empty horse trailer remaining in their caravan after a day of searching for and transporting horses, the two vets ventured to the woman's home. A sign on the fence announced: "Dogs needing to be evacuated."

Dr. Hubert is a different breed altogether. Born and raised primarily in Zimbabwe, he understands civil unrest. Guerillas had attacked his family several times while he was growing up. His aunt was among the casualties. The guerilla fighters often attacked early in the evening, giving themselves the cover of night to get away. After the first attack his family was a lot more prepared. They made sure never to have a routine. They never traveled the same road at the same time of day. Grenade screens were installed in his bedroom windows. All of his family's vehicles were equipped with roll bars and bullet proofed. Already-thick windshields were covered by mesh to protect against armor-piercing bullets.

"Not a lot of people grew up like that," Dr. Hubert said.

Needless to say, he was prepared from an early age to handle the tenuous situation Katrina had delivered. Mayhem and civil unrest were commonplace to him, but when he suggested that they take the horse trailer and evacuate forty dogs two hours after the formal curfew imposed by the National Guard, more than a few volunteers threw concerned looks his way.

At the given address was a three-story house. Despite the hurricane damage, it actually looked like a fairly nice place. It was hard to believe approximately forty dogs were inside.

The crew braced for the worst. The smells and sights of the previous rescues had torn down any inhibitions about venturing into the unknown in the hopes of saving an animal or two. Yet to their surprise, in the middle of all of the destruction and chaos, they found order. This particular house was immaculate. The dogs were all clean, and each had its own portable kennel, complete with labels and medical records.

So overwhelmed with elation that help had arrived, the woman of the house could hardly speak. After about an hour of transporting caged dogs into the horse trailer, the lady then

went through the trailer, calling each dog by name and check-
ing it off of her computer-generated list. She wanted to make
sure each one was accounted for. Her organization was amazing. She had been rescuing dogs for years and was well prepared for an emergency.

Like many others in the New Orleans area, she and her husband had refused to evacuate until their animals could be taken
as well. They were worried because they only had one small
car and a mere five gallons of gasoline. Dr. Hubert told her that
amount should be enough to get to LaPlace, but having only
loaded thirty-four dogs in the trailer, he asked what she intended
to do with the remaining six, some of which were quite large.

"Oh, these are our personal pets, and we'll just take them with
us," she replied.

"Where is your car?" Dr. Hubert inquired.

"Just there," she said, pointing to a little red Porsche.

So it was she and her husband and the remaining dogs in a
two-door sports car with barely enough gas to get to LaPlace.
The thirty-four dogs she had rescued were transported to Lamar-Dixon and handed over to the small-animal rescue agencies. They most likely were transported to Houston, where they
could then be adopted.

To date, Dr. Hubert has never heard how the woman and her
husband fared in their little fully packed red Porsche. But he
will never forget her dedication to the animals in her care and
her fierce commitment to their welfare, which was placed far
before her own.

Chapter 9

The Deluge

The floods had come. A promise made to me through a half-grinned snarl in the rearview mirror of a purple Lincoln four years earlier had come to fruition with a vengeance. Once, we had ventured into this wonderland of the Mississippi Delta for self-indulgent pursuits; now we came to help those creatures not washed away by Katrina's fury.

Each morning on our way into New Orleans, our rescue vehicles would exit Interstate 10 in LaPlace for a final fuel stop, for anything to eat, or for a restroom break. South of LaPlace was nothing but devastation.

Trash was everywhere, scattered along the roadsides and littering the streets. The outskirts of the city were now ghost towns of evacuation centers that had been staged on the edge of the flooding. The buses were gone and the people were gone, but the evidence of their hell was everywhere. Plastic grocery sacks and empty water bottles by the thousands were simply

strewn in mile-long masses of debris. Old clothes and other discarded belongings too heavy to be lugged any farther added to
the refuse: a broken bicycle, mud-caked toys, a simple wooden
chair sitting upright in the middle of the highway. It was silent
mayhem.

As the weeks wore on, the near silence might have been the
most unsettling thing of all. As we walked through the city's
once-vibrant neighborhoods in search of lost horses, we heard
only the sound of water. Water trickling from doorways, water sloshing around our feet, and water gushing from pipes as
pumps worked continuously to purge the floodwaters. Thick,
greenish-black water spewed forth with tremendous thrust
from metal pipes, at least a foot in diameter. From deep within the city straight into the troubled waters of Lake Pontchartrain, New Orleans was slowly being released from its captor's
contaminated grip, but there was nothing sweet about the
liberation.

People returning to New Orleans after Katrina were stunned
at how the city could go from a thriving metropolis to ground
zero. It looked as if someone had set off a bomb in every home
and then flushed a massive toilet over the entire thing.

After the initial shock, the numbness set in, not a physical
numbness but an almost emotional detachment from the surrounding devastation.

As we drove through a once-ordinary neighborhood a forty-
foot cabin cruiser sat atop one of the houses. No one bothered
to reach for a camera. A photographer with us said, "You know,
when you've taken a lot of pictures of all of this and you drive

past a house with a boat sticking out of the roof and you pass on the opportunity to photograph it simply because you figure you'll see something worse ... it must be pretty bad."

Roads had been ripped apart. Drivers were forced to navigate off-ramps to get on the highway and on-ramps to get off the highway; everything was backward. Residents who thought they knew how to get somewhere had to figure out an alternate route. Eyes grew wide and mouths dropped in shock at the strange sights — and then the smell hit.

The new scent of New Orleans was unlike anything any of us had experienced. It wasn't a sharp smell really, more of a heavy, putrid, deadening, oily, sewage stench born from the mixture of salt water, lake mud, silt, sewage, trash, and gas escaping from broken lines. As we were up to our knees in that goop for hours, we became very familiar with its perfume.

The devastation was depressing. The storm surge had gutted homes, leaving in its wake a flotsam of the everyday lives inside: personal belongings, groceries, furniture, family heirlooms, and children's toys, all useless and covered in mud. Despite the smell, we walked around breathing through our noses to keep anything from entering our mouths. We scrunched our faces to make our eyes and noses smaller targets. Our minds raced through our most recent vaccinations. We could recall the date of our last tetanus shot as quickly as our birth date. Every day upon finishing a given rescue attempt, we tossed contaminated hip waders into the backs of our trucks and scrubbed down with povidone-iodine right there in the street, the thick, reddish-brown lather covering our hands and forearms. The treatment was almost as disgusting as the sewage itself, but knowing it was the sanitary thing to do kept us honest when it came time to clean up and head home.

The number of ruined homes and flooded automobiles overwhelmed me. Overturned cars were piled into corners of parking lots. Evidence of civil unrest in a city completely and utterly destroyed was everywhere. An old, white mail truck sat without wheels in the middle of the interstate, huge red spray-painted graffiti covering its sides. How so much spray paint became available I will never fully understand, but every building, every shop, every home, and every office had been spray painted with hieroglyphs on the walls and doors outside. The symbols usually looked like a gigantic "X" with small numbers written in the quadrants between the lines. Usually, the figures represented the number of people found inside, the organization doing the search, the presence of dead bodies, and so forth. Bottom line, it meant someone had looked inside. What started as a simple marking method meant to identify what had been searched quickly became an unruly system of purveying information to whoever passed by. It was useful to those who understood it, I suppose, but why anyone would need to spray paint "dead dog inside" in huge orange letters across the wall of a beautiful brick home made no sense.

After a rescue mission at one farm south of New Orleans, Wallace, the LSU vet student, recalled a most unusual tale of the power and oddities of floodwaters.

"There was a brick house that just looked like it had been shaken up. You would look inside of the house and everything was upside down," he said.

The owner had informed the team that he kept some miniature horses in the back part of the property. Searching through the fields behind the home, all they found alive was one miniature horse.

Despite the catastrophic conditions some of the smallest horses and animals must have endured and the unparalleled odds stacked against them, amazingly, many of them escaped unscathed.

"It was this little bitty mini, and he was doing just fine," Wallace said.

In barns where large horses had drowned, we would often find miniature horses or small ponies still alive. Perhaps they had found better footing; perhaps they had gone along with the tide a little easier without being caught up in debris below.

"I don't know if they floated or swam," Wallace said. "But somehow they made it."

There are so many unknowns, so many unexplainable outcomes when the forces of nature spin their fortunes.

Entire houses were moved. Ships were beached in the middle of roadways miles from the river. Train cars were found straddling eight lanes of highway or sitting in the middle of fields. The whims of a hurricane were evident everywhere.

"We were looking back in a field," Wallace recalled "and [the homeowner] told me to look at this brand-new aluminum barn. Then he told me that it wasn't his. It was the whole barn, and he said that he didn't know where it came from. He had no clue."

Looking inside the barn, Wallace was surprised to discover

the interior in pristine condition. Everything was still in place. Among the contents were a new tractor and a new motorcycle that sat neatly on its kickstand. Even cans of oil and cleaning rags were sitting on the shelves, totally undisturbed, and yet the entire building was possibly miles from its original site.

"We thought that the storm must have picked up the entire barn, foundation and all, and dropped it," Wallace said.

The barn was definitely the exception to what we found on far too many occasions.

Witnessing so much wreckage and loss changes people. It changed all of us. It changed the way we felt about our own possessions. We began to think of our own homes differently. Rather than our own little places of privacy, where all of our worldly possessions are housed and where we make great dinners and have friends over, it was a shelter. Period. And it was safety. It was a place to rest so that we could go out again the next day and try to help someone else.

We opened our homes up to anyone that needed sheltering. The volunteers continually arriving from all over the country had to be housed somewhere, and usually it was in the home of someone they had barely met. After too many nights sleeping in the cabs of their trucks, they simply had to find a warm bed and a hot shower to bring a degree of normalcy to the situation. Everyone I knew at the vet school (provided their home didn't have a tree through its roof) invited someone to spend the night on the couch at some point during the rescue months.

Each evening, whether it was midnight or two in the morning, Dr. French and his wife, Nina, would bring a volunteer from

Lamar-Dixon into their home. It was often the first shower and hot meal the volunteers had had in days.

"We have beer and a bed," Nina French said. "That's our B&B."

Two volunteers, former Marines from Texas, stayed with me a few nights. I hadn't know either of them for more than ten minutes before they were both at my house — one on the couch, the other on the floor. I left the back door open so they could come and go as they pleased. Other than that first night, I never saw them again at the house although I would see evidence of their comings and goings on occasion; an empty soda can one day, an empty McDonald's bag on another. I remember that first night I woke up and left at three in the morning to serve my shift answering the hotline. These guys are ex-Marines, I thought, one little noise and they'll probably wake up. I showered, dressed, and tiptoed over them and out the door without so much as a hitch in their steady snoring.

As I drove through the dark morning, down the quiet, empty streets of Baton Rouge, I realized how quickly the oddities had become commonplace, how the chaos and change of focus had so completely enveloped everyone I knew. It seemed almost normal to have strangers living in my house, to be going to work at three in the morning, to venture southward every day in search of lost animals, and to spend my days wading through a broken city.

Chapter 10

White Horse of St. Bernard

Following the Mississippi River down past New Orleans are two parishes that share the southernmost tip of Louisiana: Plaquemines and St. Bernard. Both took a tremendous hit from Katrina. Bordered almost entirely by levees, the Mississippi River, and the gulf, they flooded like a spoon dipped into a cup of coffee. St. Bernard Parish was literally submerged. The storm surge rushed across the parish, destroying almost everything in its path. It hit with such a fury on the far side of the parish that the existing drainage pumps were damaged and useless for weeks.

At the river's edge, near the Belle Chasse ferry landing, a small convenience store, known to locals in St. Bernard simply as "the Citgo store," stood defiantly in the aftermath of the storm as a refuge for the stricken community. Louisiana native Marvin Johnson and his wife, Antonine, owned the store and had chosen to ride out the storm with their ten-year-old son, Zack.

Approximately sixty-four years old, with silver-white hair and an enduring expression of force on his weathered face, Johnson had owned the store for only two years before the hurricane. He had been an avid horseman most of his life, owning up to forty-eight racehorses at one time, running them at Fair Grounds Race Course in New Orleans. With a few horses out back, a Jack Russell, and a pet bird named Hank, Johnson and his family lived quietly just miles from the store — at least until Katrina arrived.

The flooding overtook the entire store, swamping most of the shelves and leaving a two-foot-deep lake throughout the shallow end of the parish.

In the midst of a catastrophe, when most people's minds would have turned primarily to self-preservation, Johnson immediately did what he could to provide for those who came his way. What little food he could salvage from the store he immediately gave to those who needed it.

"I didn't charge anybody anything," he recalled. "Most of my groceries and stuff, I was giving it away."

It wasn't just for those waiting for help to arrive. Johnson and his family provided food as well as shelter to countless rescuers.

"All the military was coming in here and eating. The police, the medics, they would come sleep here at night 'cause we had the generator [for the air conditioner]," he said.

When the LSU teams, including equine technicians Dawn Kelley and Leslie Talley, arrived to search for missing horses more than a week following the storms, the gas pumps in front of the store still waiting for fuel. Food and water were dwindling quickly.

Talley and Kelley are from different parts of the country and had only been working together a few months when Katrina hit, but in many ways they are cut from the same cloth. Incredibly savvy and witty, both can physically outwork most men I know and definitely were proficient in maneuvering a pickup and trailer with a load of horses through flooded terrain. With a lifetime of horse skills and a heavy dose of "no nonsense" attitude, they were the rarest kind of asset.

Knowing that her church had been very involved in caring for evacuees from New Orleans, Talley went home to Baton Rouge and asked her congregation whether it could spare any food and supplies for the people of St. Bernard Parish. The following morning when she arrived to pick up the supplies, her expectations and her vehicle were overwhelmed with a massive outpouring of food, supplies, and bottled water.

"They brought us food in all day," Johnson said. "They were the best help we had. They even gave me the little generator to run the A/C on."

For the people of St. Bernard Parish, and for victims in Slidell, Louisiana, wherever Talley went and found needs, the resources and efforts from her Baptist church soon followed. It wasn't uncommon to see Talley and Kelley go into an area with a trailer full of food and supplies and return that evening with a load of displaced animals.

With Talley's and Kelley's assistance, Johnson managed to keep his store up and running throughout the weeks following the storm. It wasn't easy. With supplies limited and assistance often deterred through bureaucratic backlog, keeping the business open was a struggle.

In the weeks following the storm, I visited Johnson's store and heard his tale.

It is a rare privilege to come face to face with individuals who have endured so much. The smallest things make the most dramatic difference: running water, chlorinated or not; lights that work without a backup generator; dry floors; clean chairs to sit on. These simple things mean so much. More than anything else though, I think Johnson was at peace just knowing he had his family together, that they had weathered yet another confrontation life was determined to deliver.

In that, Johnson was not alone.

Louis Pomes, a frequent customer at the Citgo store and a community pillar, is a lifetime native of St. Bernard Parish. He has carved out the bulk of his life on this stretch of land and knows every nook and cranny of this finger that points into the gulf. A heavy-equipment foreman for the public works department, Pomes is also a cattle farmer and a horseman. This combination of skills, experience, and community involvement led Pomes, who is in his forties, into the most demanding role imaginable when the rains and tidal surge brought on by Katrina struck his hometown.

At approximately 11:30 p.m. on August 29, the night before Katrina hit, Pomes left home to join other members of the town's public works department. They were meant to be the first responders in the area to assist with any search-and-rescue efforts following the storm. He left behind his herd of two hundred cattle and five hundred acres of lush pasture. He also left his herd of more than twenty-six horses, which he had worked years to build up. He left everything he owned to do public service.

He would never see any of his horses again. His herd of cattle would dwindle to approximately seventy, and his home would be gutted and literally drift away. Upon his return he would find it resting some seven hundred yards from its original foundation, sitting cockeyed at the bottom of his pasture.

Fourteen of his co-workers were waiting for him that evening in the town's heavy-equipment station. With eighteen-inch-thick walls built of solid mortar and rebar, the building seemed ideal for weathering heavy winds, rain, and the oncoming surge from the gulf and the river.

Arriving at the station, Pomes sloshed through waist-deep water to the front entrance.

"When I opened the door, the water came rushing in, so me and the crew, we all ran upstairs," he said. "The water came up seven feet in fifteen minutes."

Minutes later, the roof of the building blew off. The men sought refuge in the stairwell above the main floor of the building, which was now chest deep in water.

"We all spent the night there," Pomes said.

Early the next morning the town was a lake, rooftops and treetops barely visible above the water line. Determining the whereabouts of houses in residential neighborhoods would be next to impossible with the water covering street signs and other landmarks.

Despite the seeming hopelessness of the situation, the men

did the only thing that made any sense. They went in search of boats. And they found them everywhere: floating freely, tangled in debris, and caught on top of houses. When one boat ran out of fuel, they swam to another, sometimes having to hotwire them or unload them from their trailers.

"We had a lot of St. Bernard firefighters and a lot of them were also commercial fishermen, so they knew boats," Pomes recalled. "I'll never forget one boat, called *My Wife's New Car*; it was a very nice boat. Whatever woman sacrificed her new car for that boat saved a lot of lives."

They went through neighborhoods scanning the rooftops for human life, for cats or dogs. Anything living was brought out. They pounded on the roofs of homes and listened for muffled voices, a shuffle, anything that indicated life. Pomes and his teammates chopped through rooftops with axes, pulling out adults, children, and pets. People were the first priority, but animals were not left behind.

"I mean if there was an animal in distress, they came, too. If someone was on a roof with a cat, we took the cat, too. We didn't want to cause more stress," Pomes recalled.

As part of the public works department, the men had authority to attempt whatever rescues were necessary. However, they didn't subscribe to any written protocol of how these rescues were to be carried out. These weren't strange men called in to carry out a duty. This was their town. These were their people. And it was likely that on most occasions, Pomes knew the names of the people and animals he rescued. Even when it seemed that a rescue would be futile, that an animal was too far gone, they brought it out anyway. Sometimes they pushed it to high ground and let the animal have the final word on whether it was going to make it.

Pomes and the men worked for days and nights on end. The burden of responsibility, the desperation of the citizens, and the destruction of the homes in which they lived consumed them. They pressed on long after their bodies told them it was time to stop. They scrounged for food and water wherever they could find it, wading through local grocery stores and gas stations to pick up floating bottles of water and soda. Anything wrapped in plastic and floating they tore open and devoured, and on they went.

"I can remember the second day being so thirsty that I went in a Wal-Mart building and picked up floating bottles of water," Pomes said. "That's what we drank for the first couple days. We was in trouble. We ate floating food at any store. If anything floated out in a sealed bag, we ate it."

On another occasion, Pomes was lucky enough to find an old cooler still padlocked shut. After removing the padlock, he was elated to find nearly one hundred packs of frozen hotdogs inside. He took them to the fire station, where the firemen cooked them and shared them amongst the crew and any evacuees in their care. A simple thing like cooking hotdogs was a welcome feast during these times.

On the night of the storm, Pomes had two $1 bills in his front pocket. In his back pocket within his billfold was $150 in cash. For the next three months the cash sat in his wallet everywhere he went. He never spent any of it. He couldn't have had he wanted to. Its value was nothing in the situation he was in. There were no stores, no businesses, not a single establishment within twenty miles capable of taking money and providing goods or services. Not even the Citgo store.

Recalling the loose horses he gathered after the storm, Pomes was consistently impressed with the resiliency so many animals had shown. The parish president had a Welsh pony and two miniatures that Pomes was able to catch and rescue.

"I don't know how them little guys made it out of that high water, but they made it," he said. "They all shocked me that after a long swim to still be walking around after all that water we had."

Pomes continued: "You know, some of those horses that you couldn't put a halter on if you wanted to would just run up and stick their face in the halters."

The animals went wherever they were asked — into make-shift corrals, into trailers, into anything a human hand asked of them. They understood they were being helped.

Animals were anywhere dry land was to be found: on levees, on roadways, on the tops of houses, and inside buildings. They, too, had a will to endure the chaos. Regardless of their level of understanding of their predicament, they understood deep water, and they took whatever measures they could muster to survive. Some were found right back in their own pastures; no gate, no fencing, but they had either never left or they had returned. Others went where they could. Two horses were found standing side by side in front of the local feed store. As rescuers approached, the horses simply stood there, unfazed, staring at the front door of the building, as if they were reading the big white letters on a large red sign that said "Feed Store" and waiting for someone to open the door.

After days of rescuing humans, animals, and doing what he could to provide for his own survival as well, Pomes' outlook dimmed. The men on his crew were spent. Many of them had requested to leave and tend to their own troubles, see to their families, and try and regroup from the chaos and devastation. Pomes was wearing down. He was exhausted both physically and emotionally. Other than the occasional meal at the Citgo store, they had no additional support.

As the waters subsided, they found and gathered up more and more horses, more cattle, more dogs, more everything. But they had little to offer the animals other than water. Help was needed.

"I'll never forget that day that LSU came rolling in," Pomes recalled.

It was day nine following the wrath Katrina had delivered. With the situation growing bleaker by the minute, it was imperative that help arrive, and soon.

"I saw one truck and trailer come around the corner, and I thought 'thank God someone's come to help us get these horses out of here.'"

Then another one followed, and another, and another.

"It was like a big LSU convoy rolled in here," he said. "I'll tell you this ... if it hadn't been for LSU, I don't know what we'd have done."

The LSU crews spent days in the area, hauling in supplies and hauling out animals.

Pomes' own horses didn't survive. Not a single horse from his herd was ever found.

"The animals had it rough. My cattle stood in belly deep water for days. My horses never had a shot," Pomes said.

His horses had been left in their barn, safely tucked away in their stalls. But Pomes' experience would be different than that of so many of the people of New Orleans. He wouldn't return to a barn that had become a silent graveyard. Not one horse could be found anywhere, living or dead.

"I never found a horse in a stall. I think they swam over [the doors]. Once they got over them doors, they just couldn't find a place [to stand]."

They were Paint horses primarily and an occasional Quarter Horse. There were strong emotional attachments to some. Others were new additions that he was just beginning to get to know. Reflecting on the horse he had owned the longest, Pomes was quiet as he thought back on the years he had spent with a twenty-two-year-old Paint mare.

"I said I was gonna keep her until the day she died," he said, "and I did."

The most accurate description of Pomes' farm after the storm would be quiet desolation. The property basically consists of several narrow pastures that extend a half mile off the road. Several concrete pillars, about three feet high, mark where his home once stood with its manicured front yard. What little grass that remained on this sunburned and saltwater-poisoned land was brown. Fencing that surrounded the entire farm had been destroyed, either damaged beyond repair or ripped from the ground.

The trees had water stains nearly ten feet high on their trunks. They had that weary look, bending with the weather a little farther than usual. The older and larger trees had weathered similar storms; it was the younger ones that risked survival.

Remnants of farm activity were strewn throughout the property: an old broom in a ditch, a rake, empty feed sacks tangled with wire and slammed against a resisting fence post. Everything was rusty. An old saddle sat covered in mud. Undergrowth, grass, and weeds had been ripped up from the soil and thrust into every crevice of a ruined tractor. It would be a long time before Pomes' farm resembled the thriving cattle operation he once carefully tended.

Truth be told, Pomes is of St. Bernard Parish, of the soil, of the air, of the surrounding marshlands and waters as well. So much so, that I doubt he would ever leave if given the chance. Not before a storm, not during, and not after. This is home. As much as anyone's hometown is his own, so is St. Bernard to Pomes.

Daily he worked through the rubble of his community. The task was overwhelming. Cruise ships had been brought in and parked along the river's edge; a refuge for those who toiled daily in the aftermath. It was there Pomes showered and slept, unless the A/C failed and he ended up sleeping in his truck. He is trying to rebuild his life.

"I think I got about seventy left ... cows and calves together," he said. "Them girls [cows] miss me. I can get a bucket of feed, and they'll follow me anywhere. I got to be the only one who talks to cattle."

He may have been the only one talking to cattle, but he wasn't the only one talking to horses. Farther down the road lived Anna Marie Coble. In her sixties, she is a quintessential horse-woman.

"That is a lady that put more riding time on horses than any cowboy, any cowgirl you can imagine," said Pomes.

On the night of the storm, Coble scrambled to try and protect her animals. Of German descent, she was accustomed to hard work, long hours in the saddle. The smile on her weathered tan face shows the years of dedication and satisfaction. When the waters pushed higher than anticipated, Coble saw one of her horses fighting through the surge. Seeing it caught in a wave, she hoped it would push all the way to the levee and eventually find dry ground. At the height of the storm, there was little she could actually do. With her home being swallowed by floodwaters and the rains continuing to pelt down, she felt helpless as she watched her animals being swept away — until she thought of the bridge.

Just down the road from her home in St. Bernard was Violet Bridge. It is a small bridge compared to those that span the Mississippi, but it arches up and over Violet Canal giving it enough height that she felt surely the waters would never be able to submerse it. With her prized black-and-white Paint horse in tow, she pushed through waist-deep floodwaters toward the bridge, her short white hair plastered to her head from the driving rain. When they arrived, she was elated to find that while the waters were deep on either side, the bridge sat high out of harm's way. It was the ideal place, in her mind, to leave her horse safe from the rising water all around.

She left her beloved Paint horse there, and in the days that followed the storm, she would make frequent trips to bring him hay and see to his well being. The horse wasn't tied, but left to roam back and forth on the bridge at will, corralled by flood-waters. Throughout the days spent rescuing citizens, Pomes would see the horse whenever he passed the area. Coble had been forced to evacuate but had left word on the whereabouts of her horse, and frequently rescuers would bring him hay and take care of him. Pomes and his comrades even built a temporary shelter in the middle of the bridge out of boards and an old tarp, so that the horse could seek shade when the blistering sun became too much to bear.

Wandering down to water's edge and waiting, he was a common sight to many of the rescuers. And to Pomes, it was nice to be able to come and visit him from time to time and put his hands on a healthy horse once again.

Talley recalled the day Coble returned to get her horse from Violet Bridge. Looking forward to being reunited with her horse, she had arrived at Lamar-Dixon very early, even before anyone else had gotten there. When rescuers began to assemble for the day's search, Coble asked if she could ride along to get her horse. She also inquired whether any of the LSU rescuers had seen the horse recently. A local volunteer rolled by in an open top jeep, towing a small flat boat. The LSU team asked him whether he had seen Coble's horse lately.

Chapter 10

"Oh, the horse on the bridge?" he said. "Yeah, somebody shot it."

The group fell silent.

"What?" Coble said.

Just then Pomes rolled up in a borrowed truck.

"Louis, we need to go see my horse," Coble exclaimed "Take me to the bridge … I can't believe someone would shoot it! There was nothing wrong with that horse!

"Who would shoot my horse!" she cried as she ran around to the other side of Pomes' truck and climbed inside.

They found her beloved horse, lying dead in the middle of Violet Bridge from a fatal gunshot wound to the head. Coble knelt down, examined the bullet wound, was silent for a long time, and then got up and walked back to the truck. She did what she had always done. She moved on.

She immediately turned her efforts to trying to do some good. She returned to the LSU team and continued helping rescue horses for the rest of the day. It was the day that her horse should have been on an LSU trailer headed for Lamar-Dixon. But a beautiful black-and-white horse that had endured a week of hurricane aftermath alone on Violet Bridge would not be among those rescued that day. It was a loss Coble will never forget or any of us ever understand.

Contemplating on Coble's loss, his own situation, and looking to the future, Pomes pondered taking back what the storm has claimed.

"I ain't gonna get more than two more horses," he concluded, "that's all I'm gonna wind up with. Just in case I have a riding buddy to go out with ... But I have to have a horse; it's in my blood."

***

On October 27, 2005, at the Breeders' Cup championship races, run that year at Belmont Park in Elmont, New York, an award known throughout the equine industry as simply the "White Horse Award" was presented. This tribute is sponsored by the Race Track Chaplaincy of America to honor and celebrate those in the equine industry who have gone the extra mile in service of others. Annually, nominees are submitted for heroic acts at racetracks and farms throughout America, for going beyond the call of duty to save lives or eliminate danger. In a marquee tent, next to the paddock at New York's storied racetrack, Hall of Fame jockey Pat Day presented the White Horse Award to the 2005 recipient, Louis Pomes of St. Bernard, Louisiana.

Chapter 11

Duncan

Right after the storm, a gentleman from Oregon began calling our hotline. He needed our help finding a horse his daughter was boarding at a stable on Haynes Boulevard near Lake Pontchartrain. His daughter Kristin, who had recently relocated from Oregon to New Orleans to attend Tulane University, was an avid equine enthusiast. She had taken her prized gelding, Duncan, along to compete in collegiate hunter/jumper events. Duncan was a star. He and Kristin had earned countless ribbons together.

Kristin had been in the city only a couple of weeks when Katrina's impending landfall forced her and her classmates to evacuate. As she fled the city, her Northwestern roots undoubtedly gave her little understanding of a hurricane's potential. And even if she had grasped the threat, she had no means of taking her horse with her.

It wasn't that she didn't care. She cared very deeply. But like so many other horse owners in the area, she left believing that Duncan would be safe from the storm at his stable, where he resided with more than seventy other horses, each professionally groomed and attended to daily.

When the storm hit, Duncan and his stablemates were carefully tucked in their stalls, out of harm's way from the driving rain, the hundred-mile-per-hour winds, and the onslaught of flying debris. But much of the tidal surge from Lake Pontchartrain and the eventual breaches of inner-city canals throughout the area wreaked absolute havoc along Haynes Boulevard, submerging neighborhoods and engulfing the stable where Duncan was boarded.

When Kristin's father got news of the situation, he called relentlessly from Oregon about his daughter's beloved horse.

"Sir, I'm sorry, but we've been down in that area as far as we can go, and it's absolutely impassable," I told him again and again.

We had attempted several times to access the area, as Duncan wasn't the only "unknown" on the list in the Haynes Boulevard area. The waters, exceeding fifteen feet, were simply too high. We had canoes, or "pirogues" as they are known in Cajun country, but we still had no access to motorboats, and it is literally impossible to swim a horse and paddle a canoe simultaneously. And while we knew the horses' last-known addresses, the high water made it impossible to determine exact locations in the drift of contamination floating above all the remaining street signs.

His calls continued.

Chapter 11

"Why can't you get a boat in there and take a look around ... He [Duncan] probably made it and just needs feed and water; can you at least get in and leave feed and water?"

He wouldn't let up. He called nearly every thirty minutes for days, receiving the same answer time after time.

"I'm not answering that phone again," someone yelled during the height of the calling frenzy as the pressure and stress of the effort continued to heighten our frustrations. We knew it was him, and he refused to take no for an answer.

He wasn't the only one. With nothing to go by other than the images shown on CNN and with whirlwinds of unknowns swirling in their minds, the callers had but one option that hinted of result: Call LSU. And call they did. Just like Kristin's father, they called nonstop, often challenging our responses. There *had* to be something we could do, *anything*.

Every day we continued to try and get into the area. I gave Kristin's father my cell phone number so I could give him the most recent information we had. We went to the water's edge and we waded in; we searched, we whistled, we tore up trucks, and we blew countless tires driving through the unending sea of trash cluttering the storm-ravaged roadways or what was left of them. We searched as far as we could go. We found nothing.

He phoned again.

"Can't you get a helicopter and get in there and take a look around," he pleaded.

I informed him that obtaining a Black Hawk to look for one horse when so many people remained stranded in the city would be nearly impossible.

He phoned again.

"Listen," he said, "I have personally hired a helicopter and pilot out of Baton Rouge who has agreed to fly into that area. If one of you will go with him and look for Duncan, I would greatly appreciate it."

I thought about it for a moment. We discussed it as a group.

"We'll do it," I told him. "Just tell us where to meet the chopper, and we'll go and try again."

At the last moment, though, the pilot refused the mission. We searched for another solution and called a pilot in the National Guard who is the brother of Dr. Ashley Stokes, one of our vets. He was flying human-rescue missions in New Orleans and had an aerial view of the area and the water levels.

"It's too high," he reported back to us. "Everything is still underwater, and I don't see anything on the levees right now ... no animals of any kind."

The outlook was dim. I answered the phone again. "We can't make it in there. We are simply going to have to wait until the water goes down and then get in as far as we can."

Kristin's father refused to give up. He was polite, but he wasn't patient. He continued to call each day to check on our progress, to hear our descriptions, and to update the picture of the situation in his mind's eye.

Every day the little red arrows on our wall map would change. Only one stayed constant. It was Duncan's arrow, and though we still couldn't access his area, we never forgot his last-known location. We were thrust into a world of the "missing." And the toll of the unknown was probably as difficult as facing the

Although the roof and some walls remained standing, the interior of this barn in Jefferson Parish was totally destroyed.

Miraculously, this barn did not totally collapse; the debris caught above the stall dividers shows how high the water rose.

A band of horses spotted by a helicopter reconnaissance mission in lower Plaquemines Parish three weeks after Hurricane Katrina. These horses were grazing on the levee, the only available dry land remaining near the mouth of the Mississippi River.

A map-covered blackboard at LSU's Horse Hurricane Helpline in Baton Rouge. Each red arrow represented the last known location of a missing horse.

KY MORTENSEN PHOTOS

The chalkboard at the Horse Hurricane Helpline center at the LSU School of Veterinary Medicine displayed the many names and contact numbers of those who assisted with the equine hurricane rescue effort.

In the days following Hurricane Katrina, we saw messages like these everywhere, as rescuers used them to communicate with each other. We called it "Katrinage."

Dr. Shannon Gonsoulin comforts a traumatized horse found in a ruined stable near Haynes Boulevard a few blocks from Lake Pontchartrain.

Dr. Shannon Gonsoulin (right) and Dr. Jeff Artall use a makeshift lead to coax a mud-caked horse through neighborhood ruins near Haynes Boulevard in east New Orleans.

Dr. Gonsoulin prepares his tranquilizer gun in east New Orleans. While firearms were often carried for personal protection, tranquilizer guns also were occasionally used to assist in the capture of unfriendly dogs or unruly horses.

This miniature horse and two ponies were rescued near Haynes Boulevard. Their elderly caretaker had managed to supplement them with Red Cell, a sugar-infused, vitamin-mineral supplement. This, in addition to a small flood-damaged backyard pasture, was all the horses had to eat. Surprisingly, the mini was not in poor condition. Inset, Dr. Dennis French, attending veterinarian at Lamar-Dixon.

Above, Marvin Johnson and his family relax in their Citgo store. For many weeks, their store in the heart of St. Bernard Parish supplied food, shelter, and hope. Below, fishing and recreational boats litter Louisiana Highway 23 near Venice, Louisiana, in Plaquemines Parish.

Although our primary focus was the rescue of equines, we managed to save a fair number of goats, dogs, cats — even a bird or two. Note the Humvee in the background; by this point, New Orleans was under military supervision.

Most horses, even terribly traumatized horses, loaded immediately into a trailer. But, sometimes, a little negotiation was needed.

We often used a long rope tied to the trailer to bring a horse's haunches around to encourage it to load. For really reluctant loaders, we some-times used "liquid rope" — a sedative.

Above and facing page, many bodies were found like this, almost as if they had been gently set down as the water receded around them. In the heat and humidity, decomposition set in rapidly.

Every horse, living and dead, was scanned for the presence of a microchip. To prepare for emergencies, all horse owners should consider having their horses implanted with microchips.

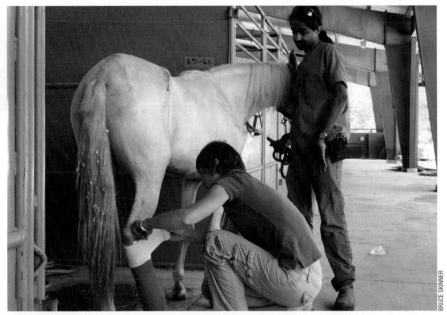

LSU veterinary student Ashok Padmanabhon and a volunteer treat a horse with a leg wound. Leg wounds, skin abrasions, and skin conditions were fairly common, given the environments in which we found many horses.

Lucien Mitchell Jr. at the Lamar-Dixon Expo Center with Tootsie, one of the mules from the Charbonnet Mid-City Carriage Company. Mitchell repeatedly refused to evacuate in order to stay with the mules.

Sharon Williams was happily reunited with her Quarter Horse gelding Flash at the Lamar-Dixon Expo Center nearly a month after Hurricane Katrina. Flash had been rescued from the floodwaters of St. Bernard Parish.

RUSTIN MOORE

BRUCE SKINNER

From left, a group shot of author Ky Mortensen, Dr. Shannon Gonsoulin, volunteer Phil Saboy, Dr. Dina Duplantis, and Phil's wife taken in east New Orleans Parish.

Molly, a Pony of the Americas mare, survived an attack by a pit bull after Hurricane Katrina. When the only option to save her life was to amputate her leg to stop a lethal infection, Molly was given an experimental, prosthetic leg. Miraculously, it worked and Molly survived.

KJ MORTENSEN

flooding itself; even more so for Kristin and her family as they struggled each waking hour with thoughts of "what if."

We will probably never know exactly what Duncan and his stablemates endured during the height of the storm and subsequent flooding. But based on the experiences of many horses in barns and stables throughout southern Louisiana during this time, he likely faced a trial similar to that of other horses locked in their stalls during Katrina.

Had they lived in a more rural setting, they likely would have been turned out into their pasture, even during the worst of the storm, as this would have ensured their greatest chance for survival. But the middle of New Orleans doesn't have a lot of open range, and residents had no way of knowing the floodwaters were coming. They expected winds and they expected rain, and with those thoughts in mind, the most prudent precaution was to keep animals inside. But flooding is a different beast.

Marks in several barns examined after the floods showed the water had risen well above ten to fifteen feet. While many horses were found drowned, a surprising number actually survived.

As we entered barns after the storm, we would often find miniature horses and small ponies standing in the breezeway completely out of their stalls. The only explanation for this is that the smaller horses were actually swept up and over their stall doors and simply swam around the barn until the water subsided enough for them to gain solid footing.

The larger horses either broke free, or they swam in their stalls, or they died. They treaded water for hours, perhaps even days, and they literally tore the flooring out of their stalls as their legs constantly churned against the tide and they fought to keep their heads above water.

I will never forget seeing the padlocked stall doors with dead horses behind them. As we entered barns in the parishes of Plaquemines, St. Bernard, and East Orleans, time and time again we would find the entrances heavily barred. Whether these barns were in shambles, barely clinging to their foundations, or steadfastly holding their ground, the outcome for the prized lives contained within was too often the same. The horses were trapped with water rising by the minute. They could swim; they could attack the walls; they could fight in any way possible. But for days, with flooding preventing access, no humans could provide help. If a horse were to survive, it would likely do so by its own conviction, its own unwillingness to surrender to the surge that had consumed the safest place it knew. Many survived doing just that: swimming and fighting until the water relented. Sadly, others did not.

As I stood in the breezeway of one flood-ravaged barn, it seemed like a bad dream. Hay and trash were slammed against one end of the barn. Corroded padlocks still were fastened to crumbling stall doors. Not a horse was in sight. And then inside the stalls was the unthinkable: drowned horses, lying in mud, bloated and rotting. Owners had thought they were doing what was best for their horses. No one knew the flooding would occur, and no one knew when they'd be able to return to their homes, thus the volume of calls to LSU for help and the pleas to search on their behalf.

Perhaps the most horrific image I witnessed was only through a photograph. Dr. Allison Barca, a veterinarian whose practice and clinic are in New Orleans proper, spent days after the hurricane going from farm to farm, from house to house, to check on her clients' horses. She had photographed hundreds of ruined barns, smashed houses, and horses that had not survived. I have forgotten most of them as they all seem to run together into one mass grave in my mind. But one image stands alone. It was a photo of a horse that had escaped his stall into the confines of his barn during the flood surge. Whether he had broken the door down or swam over the top is unknown. Either way, he had made it into the main breezeway that divided the rows of stalls. An electric hoist hung from the ceiling of the barn, far overhead, fastened to the rafters with chains. No doubt it was used to offload heavy bundles of hay and supplies or to work on the occasional tractor engine. Like any other hoist, it operated on a system of pulleys, and two loops of chain hung down, one about three feet, the other extending nearly to the floor.

As this horse fought the tidal surge within his barn, pushing against the water and swimming against the current to keep his head above the contamination, the upward force of the water thrust him into the hoist. He became entangled in the chains, his head locked in the smaller loop, which now claimed his lifeless body like an unforgiving hangman's noose. He had struggled right there, thrashing in the tide and the chains until his burning lungs flooded with water, and he was gone.

As the waters slowly receded around him, the weight of his corpse gave way to gravity, and as decomposition ensued during the following days, his hide draped from his head to the floor like a magnificent robe extending all around. It is one of the most gruesome images I have ever beheld.

There was life and there was death. In Plaquemines Parish, cows were seen hanging lifeless twenty feet above the ground, caught in tree branches. And twenty-four miles from the mouth of Vermilion Bay, a small black cow was found standing alone on the base platform of a drifting oil rig, her coat dry as a bone, her physical condition superb, calmly chewing her cud, staring out at the endless sea, in the middle of the Gulf of Mexico.

Imagine the power these creatures had endured, the sheer forces of nature, sweeping them along like leaves in a raging river. Imagine the one thought that consumed every cell in their minds: swim.

Duncan swam. How long he fought against the contaminated filth that inundated his stall, we will never know. He likely broke the door down, and whether he attacked his confines and fought his way to freedom, or whether his barn was destroyed and he swam through the wreckage, one thing is certain ... he swam. The area where he was housed left him no other option. The water was simply too deep. Through wind and rain, through darkness and debris, and with that innate ability to find dry land that animals have, Duncan fought a force of nature he had never before seen. Born into the clean misty rains of Oregon and the pampered life of a show horse, he was now forced to face the awesome sludge, the screaming winds, and the unfathomable tide of Hurricane Katrina. But Duncan swam. He swam and he fought and he kept on swimming. And he made it.

He, along with a handful of other horses, either from his own stable or from stables nearby, was found on the levee that was the only dry land separating Lake Pontchartrain from the lake that was now New Orleans. There he was, though nobody at the time knew it was him.

I was not present on the levee that day. Dr. Shannon Gonsoulin, along with other LSU team members and a slew of volunteers, finally had made his way onto Haynes Boulevard on day ten. Duncan was simply one horse among a group of horses gathered up that day in the LSU net. After being housed at Lamar-Dixon for a few days, his sun-bleached coat no longer matched the photos Kristin had e-mailed to Dr. Rusty Moore. But his markings and the distinctive scar on his forehead matched the description closely enough to cause us to take a second look. It was Duncan, sure enough.

A phone call informed Kristin and her father. Probably through tears, lingering doubts, fear of another disappointment, and an underlying hint of "please, God, let it be him," she came to be reunited with her horse. Exactly how he survived, we will never know; but Duncan made it, and he was headed home to Oregon.

To see things come full circle is a rare opportunity. Often during the mayhem of daily operations, it is easy to lose sight of the real reason for a given task. To be honest, in many instances our efforts seemed incredibly futile. To think that jotting down the requests, descriptions, and directions of a horse owner now hundreds of miles away was going to make any sense once we got down into New Orleans was truly difficult to believe. Particularly when the city had been turned upside down and covered in water.

Depending on whether there was cell phone service, rescue teams would occasionally update us throughout the day. Often, however, we wouldn't know a rescue attempt's outcome until the teams returned at nightfall. The information would be compiled in a report so that by the following day everyone knew where everything stood. It was a great time of day when those rescue reports came in. Manning the phones for hours, we could easily lose that connection with the realities occurring just an hour south of us. Hearing the results and seeing the fruits of our labors, so to speak, were something all of us looked forward to.

Like most other callers, a woman I spoke to one evening went into great detail about the location of her horses, their breeding, size, and color, along with a description of her home in Chalmette. As usual, I wrote down exactly what she said.

Like so many others before, this woman had evacuated, leaving enough feed and water for her horses to get by for a few days. Three days, to be exact. She then learned that the area in which she lived had flooded and it might be months before she could return to what was left of her home. As she described her horses, her address, her house color, and the multiple methods of entry into her neighborhood, she paused for a second and then said, "Do you all only go after horses, or can you help small animals as well?"

I told her that our primary focus was horses but we had assisted with small-animal efforts, depending on the circumstances and our ability to help.

"Well, I have this cat," she said. "You can't catch him or anything, but I wondered if you might leave him some food?"

My eyes started to roll. It would be a miracle if her house was even accessible, much less that her horses would still be where she left them, and even more so a miracle if we were able to locate a feral cat that supposedly lived somewhere on the premises.

"OK," I continued. "Tell me about the cat."

The cat lived pretty much wherever he wanted, and the woman had kind of adopted him over the years. He came and went as he pleased, and she had never actually caught him, but he usually lived in the storage room at the top of her house. It was an old apartment she had turned into a makeshift workshop and storage area. There was a staircase alongside the house, right between the horses' paddock and her home. It was a white staircase and white house. The stairs went up to the workshop entrance, and the cat often could be found inside.

"I think if it has flooded, he'll most likely be there," she said.

I jotted down the information in barely legible format, noting the information on the horses and then included the story about the cat.

I don't know if I had become overly doubtful simply due to the nonstop bad news we kept hearing about the situation in New Orleans or if ten straight hours of answering phone calls had left me less than enthusiastic, but I had my doubts about these horses, and I would have bet money we couldn't check on this cat.

I wrote it all down anyway. The cat was supposed to be in the apartment; the key was at the top of the stairs under the doormat. We weren't to retrieve the cat as that would likely be impossible, but if we could leave some cat food inside the door, it would be much appreciated. Those were my very instructions. It was almost humorous as I jotted them all down. I was sure whoever would read them the following day would be elated at the tedious manner in which I had spelled out this particular rescue attempt.

About six o' clock each morning, crews would line up convoy style to receive their instructions for the day. Each crew would be assigned to an area based on information we had gathered from the previous day's calls and reconnaissance. We would go from cab to cab of each pickup, trailer in tow, and give each driver a master list of all the rescues, with his own responsibilities marked in bold letters. As the drivers looked down the sheet, scanning the information, they would figure out the materials needed and gather what was necessary from our now-awesome stock of donated supplies. Some areas were heavily flooded and would require canoes or waders or both. Often crews would need to deliver hay and supplies to farms along the way.

As the crew headed to Chalmette read through its list with my information, they didn't think twice. They marched over to the small-animal rescue barn and asked for a bag of cat food.

"Forget why or how; in fact, don't ask us anything about what we're doing. We just need some cat food."

They threw the bag into the back of the truck along with halters, ropes, and waders, and off they went. It was almost comical, venturing off into the unknown with very little idea of whether we could even access these areas. We had so little in-group PETA (People for the Ethical Treatment of Animals). As Dr. Pugh readied his equipment and materials for performing the procedure, he asked one of the veterinary students to hold a twitch on the horse while he worked. A twitch is basically a three-foot-long wooden staff with a small loop of cotton rope on the end. The loop is placed around the horse's top lip. The wooden handle is then twisted to tighten the loop around the lip. In defense of the onlookers, it can appear to be painful, but a great deal of science stands behind the procedure.

As the small noose tightened around the stallion's lip and Dr. Pugh began his work, one onlooker had tolerated all he possibly could.

"I am going to have to ask you to remove that device," he said.

Dr. Pugh emerged from under the horse's belly.

"And why is that?" he asked.

"I am a representative from PETA, and I am interfering on behalf of the humane treatment of this animal."

"Oh, you are?" asked Dr. Pugh.

"Yes," replied the man, "that device is causing pain, it is unnecessary, it is inhumane, and on behalf of this animal, I am interfering, and I want that device removed."

"Do you know what that device is?" asked Dr. Pugh.

"No," the man replied.

"It's called a twitch," Dr. Pugh replied.

"I don't care what it is called; I want it removed," the man said.

"Why do you think it is inhumane?" asked Dr. Pugh.

"Because you're twisting it really tight, and it looks like it probably hurts," the man answered.

Dr. Pugh continued, "This device, known as a twitch, is applying pressure to the nerve endings in this horse's nose. By doing so, it releases chemical signals into the horse's brain, causing a relaxing effect and a naturally induced semi-sedated state. The horse is not in pain; he is relaxed. If he were in pain, he would fight back or offer some sort of resistance. He may even make a noise. He's not making a noise. He's not doing anything but standing there completely relaxed so that I can safely do my work."

The man abandoned his accusations and offered no further disagreement. Dr. Pugh returned to his work, and the man stayed to observe the procedure. The stallion was treated. The conversation was over.

Chapter 14

The Arkansas Herd

As calls continued jamming the Horse Hurricane Helpline, we often were confronted with individuals looking for immediate action. Either they had seemingly figured out exactly where their horse was located in New Orleans and needed us to send someone to get it that very instant or they had other plans that required our urgent assistance.

Every so often, immediate action was actually possible. Most times, however, it was not. It took a mountain of coordination, equipment, and manpower to carry out a well-planned rescue mission, much less to respond instantly to a specific call. We also had the added challenge of dwindling volunteers combined with the sheer distance and time necessary to reach rescue areas and complete the assigned work before dark. Perhaps unaware of what they were asking, our callers typically didn't care for any answer other than yes.

About a week after Katrina hit, we received a call from an Ar-

137

kansas "rescue organization" we had heard neither of nor from before. They relayed a detailed account of an equine rescue effort they had attempted that day in New Orleans and then asked us to help them finish the job. Apparently, they had worked their way down into New Orleans with a pickup and horse trailer full of their own horses. Having made their base camp at Harrah's Casino in the middle of downtown New Orleans, they had set out on horseback to gather wandering animals. From what we could determine, no one asked them to do this, nor had anyone really given them permission. But given the sheer calamity of the situation, operating without official permission wasn't that unusual. Throughout the day they had supposedly ridden the flooded streets of New Orleans gathering a stray mule here and a wandering carriage horse there, and had taken the entire herd back to their base camp to transport them out of the city. However, there wasn't enough room for all of the animals in their trailers. Five mules and two horses had been left behind for the LSU crew to come get. The Arkansas rescue group had cornered the animals near the tracks of the downtown trolley and had corralled them in a makeshift enclosure of empty fifty-five gallon drums in an alleyway just past the Aquarium of the Americas right next to the Mississippi River in downtown New Orleans. At least that was what they said.

About 4:30 p.m., we learned of the necessary mission into New Orleans. Downtown New Orleans was roughly an hour away and curfew there was 6 p.m. Also, darkness would be approaching by the time any team could reach the designated area where the horses and mules were believed to be temporarily contained.

The day had already been long. I had taken more calls that day by the end of my twelve-hour stint, than I will even be able to recall accurately. And now we were hearing from the Arkansas round-up crew. I announced the situation to anyone within earshot.

"Can we do this?" I asked. "Do we have anyone or anything that we can go and get these horses with?"

We discussed it for a few minutes, looking on our map at the area we believed the horses were. The call sounded very convincing. If no one went immediately, the horses would more than likely escape or possibly be taken by anyone happening to wander by. Would it be the end of the world if we didn't get down there and get these horses that very instant? Probably not, but knowing now that we had a small crew and a vehicle available, we decided it was a mission we could undertake at that moment.

It made little sense then, and even less looking back on it now, but be that as it may, Dr. Dan Burba from our LSU team agreed to go get these horses and mules. He contacted John Ladner, a local vet tech and volunteer who had a pickup and a trailer, and the two headed for New Orleans. They took along their own firearms as well. They would be entering some of the most heavily populated areas of New Orleans and, at the time, some of the most dangerous.

As Dr. Burba and Ladner ventured southward, they met up and convoyed with the two ex-Marines who had been staying at my house. We had quickly learned that the best system for searching flooded areas for lost horses was with two or more vehicles, preferably one without a trailer in tow. Searching in this fashion, the "free" vehicle can better maneuver through and around obstacles and find the best route for the trucks pulling the trailers.

As the team scanned the city from atop the interstate, the flooding became very real and a feeling of uneasiness set in as they searched for a possible exit into the deluge and toward the section of town where we thought the horses were.

Dr. Burba radioed back to me at headquarters in Baton Rouge.

"This isn't going to work," he said. "Elysian Fields is completely under water."

They had resumed driving and were in downtown New Orleans. The military was everywhere, roads were blocked, floodwaters were all around, and guns were being fired.

I searched the map on the wall at headquarters for the best possible route to get them where they needed to be. I radioed back, naming possible alternative streets.

As Dr. Burba and his team progressed through the city, they were met at gunpoint by a SWAT team from North Carolina. Fully decked out in SWAT attire and MP-5 machine guns, the group requested identification and demanded to know their business. When Dr. Burba explained what they were trying to do, they lowered their guns, allowing the rescue team to proceed to the next checkpoint.

The roads they traversed were harrowing. Garbage was everywhere, roadblocks appeared out of nowhere for no apparent reason, and despite Dr. Burba's best attempts to maneuver the truck and trailer through the maze, he was driving in circles and making little progress.

"How far down on Elysian Fields are they?" he radioed me.

I was going off of the memory of a fifteen-second and frequently interrupted phone call I had had an hour beforehand.

"I'm not sure. I think you just keep going until you come to the river; there are supposed to be some stables or a barn or something near the aquarium right at the railroad tracks before you get to the river," I replied.

"So do I stay on Elysian or just go to the river?" he shot back.

"Just go to the aquarium or as close as you can get and radio back when you get there."

I could hear the chaos on his end. The uneasiness in his voice was an indication of his surroundings. He sounded stressed and rushed, as if he were running from something or to something. It was obvious the latter, yet from his tone you couldn't be sure.

I was trying to figure the whole thing out. I phoned the Arkansas rescue group again, but they had long since left the city and were headed back to Baton Rouge.

"Where exactly are the mules, and why didn't you just load them up when you found them? Were there too many?" I asked.

"We don't have another trailer," one of the men replied. "We went down into the city this morning and spent all day on horseback rounding up loose horses and mules. We cornered them all in an empty lot by the aquarium and locked them in by stacking barrels and debris around the entrance. Just tell your man to keep looking. They're there."

I radioed Dr. Burba and crew and let them know what I knew, which at that point wasn't really much. Dr. Burba was driving for all he was worth trying to do the best he could. He came back on the radio "OK, I'm on the street [Elysian Fields Avenue] tell me where to turn and how far down they are … this is crazy down here. We need to find these mules as quick as we can and get out of here."

I glanced again at the map and raced to the computer to see what roads appeared to still be open. "Can you see the aquarium yet?" I asked.

"Hold on, I think we found them," he replied.

It was silent for what seemed like an eternity.

"They're here alright," he said. "I thought you said they were in a barn."

The animals were in a dirt lot next to a lumberyard, far down the road from the aquarium, near the French Market next to the Quarter. The lot, which appeared to be a loading dock behind some warehouses, was basically empty, other than the mules and horses. There were metal buildings all around, and a bunch of old black metal barrels had been stacked to block the exit, temporarily keeping the animals contained. They could have easily toppled them over and escaped, but they simply hadn't been there long enough to figure it out.

As Dr. Burba approached, he heard a shout from way off. "What do you all think you're doing?" Dr. Burba glanced at Ladner, and they both looked back at the two ex-Marines who had accompanied them. They were volunteers from Texas who had simply arrived to help with the cause, but at that moment, Dr. Burba was glad to have someone on his team who had military experience.

Dr. Burba circled but couldn't see anything or anyone. He neared the small herd, which was clumped together in one corner. Three horses and two mules, none of which had halters on. He was going to have to catch them one by one. The first one appeared to be an easy catch, but anyone who has ever tried to catch a herd of horses knows that when one tries to escape, they all take off in different directions.

A voice was heard again. Ladner, who had remained with the truck, leaned his shotgun against the horse trailer so as not to appear overly threatening but so that anyone nearby would see they were armed. A small man whose hair had gone white with age approached.

"Thank you so much for coming to get my mules," he said. "These are my mules from my carriage business. I can take care of myself, but I can't look after these mules right now."

And then he disappeared.

Darkness began to fall and shadows from the tall city buildings consumed the streets. A rising level of angst pushed the crew to hurry. After several attempts they caught another mule. After haltering it, they used it as both bait and a shield as Dr. Burba neared the rest of the herd and put his arm around the neck of another horse. They continued in this fashion until all but one of the mules were loaded onto the trailer. Dr. Burba made his way back into the alley. The mule was running wild, jumping over barrels, crashing through debris. With shots being fired throughout the day, no fresh water to be found, and constant helicopter traffic overhead, the animal was in no mood to be friendly, and the thought of packing himself into a loaded trailer was not very high on his agenda.

A convoy of police cars sped through the neighborhood, right past the truck and trailer. They were headed out of the neighborhoods, back to base camp at Harrah's for the night. It was no time to be out and alone in New Orleans. It was no time to be chasing a mule down a darkened street. It took a little "cowboying," but the mule finally was herded into a corner, where the crew could get a halter on him.

Loaded and headed home, Dr. Burba contacted me on the radio. "We got 'em." That was all he said before signing off.

An hour later Dr. Burba arrived at Lamar-Dixon and so began the retelling of tales of SWAT teams and shots fired, of a deserted city and massive heaps of rubble. For those of us who hadn't yet been into this section of the city, the story was met with great amazement and countless questions. It was a job well done. And while it was a great effort for a few stray horses and mules, it was yet one more example of the willingness of crews and volunteers to respond to the needs of the equine community. But above all, it was a safe retreat for three horses and two mules that would spend the remainder of their Katrina days at Lamar-Dixon before returning home to New Orleans after peace and running water had been restored.

Chapter 15

The Candy Man's Mule

Early one morning a group of veterinarians and students from LSU made its way into New Orleans to check on several carriage stables in the inner city and near the French Quarter.

Designed for tourists, wedding parties, and an occasional Sunday afternoon outing, carriage rides are big business in New Orleans. Before Katrina more than twelve such companies did business in the city, each with half a dozen carriages and approximately twenty or more horses and mules.

Armed with halters, hip waders, and canoes, the group was going to try to reach several of these stables previously off-limits because of high water.

Its first stop was The Roaring Twenties, a typical carriage stable that contained a small herd. These horses pulled beautifully decorated and sometimes elaborate carriages through the French Quarter, along St. Charles Avenue, and throughout other picturesque areas of the city.

After strapping on hip waders and organizing the halters and leads, the group trudged through the knee-deep waters toward the stables, located just fifty meters off of Interstate 10. The barn roof had been completely blown off, and the building overall was pretty dilapidated. It took four of our men to knock down the locked gate. Inside, the mules, also knee-deep in water, were pretty fractious because of all the helicopters hovering overhead for the past week. They crashed around in the water, banging up the stalls, kicking sideboards, and basically demonstrating their unwillingness to be caught.

In addition to the air traffic above, a large number of people were being evacuated from the nearby streets.

"They were still picking up people on the side of us with helicopters, making a hell of a noise," Dr. Shannon Gonsoulin said. "We had a few halters and one or two lead ropes, and there were like eighteen mules we had to catch. And some of these mules were big mules."

Remarkably, when rescuers would put their hands on them, the animals usually would immediately calm down.

"It was almost as if they knew that you were going to rescue them," Dr. Gonsoulin said.

The crew had haltered a few mules and had begun to make its way back to the interstate. Dr. Randy Hayes was a volunteer on that trip. An LSU grad, Dr. Hayes is a veterinarian who worked with Dr. Gonsoulin in his New Iberia practice; Dr. Hayes is big, about 6 feet and 200 pounds, and a powerhouse when it comes to handling unruly horses. He was leading a fairly large mule that he wanted to get through the water, up the off ramp onto dry land, and to the trailer. A vet student stood waiting to assist him at water's edge. Just as Dr. Hayes neared the trailer, a helicopter flew by and the mule started dancing around and splashing contaminated floodwater everywhere.

"When I looked back again, all I could see was that mule running down the off ramp of I-10 without Randy," said Dr. Gonsoulin, who had returned to fetch more mules by that time.

When the runaway mule returned to the ruined barn that had been his home, he was cornered again, caught, and given back to Dr. Hayes. His captivity did not last long. The crew's final view of the mule was his hindquarters as he ran free, headed down Orleans Avenue.

Times like these bring things into perspective. We might have been doing what is necessary after a catastrophic natural disaster, and some of us might have been educated men and women with several letters behind our names, but there came moments when we were face to face with a mule covered in crap that simply didn't want to ride in the same truck with us and we couldn't do a thing about it.

In the middle of one of these enlightening moments, a man near the water's edge at the bottom of the off ramp asked to borrow one of the canoes. He wanted to retrieve family members who lived nearby. Dr. Gonsoulin agreed and went along to help. The man's mother, along with his two brothers, was stranded down the flooded street.

"We loaded everything they had into two canoes," Dr. Gonsoulin said, "and all his mother brought was this little Winn-Dixie [grocery] bag full of stuff … that was it."

"It was heartbreaking because you saw people leaving everything they had," he continued.

Moving through flooded areas, we saw just how much people had lost. But we didn't experience it as they had. We hadn't lost our homes, our livelihoods, and all of our treasured belongings. We were there to gather lost animals. It was different when we encountered human evacuees who desperately needed a helping hand. Seeing their lives brutally disrupted and looking at the cost of the experience written in the lines of their faces brought things clearly into perspective.

"That was the reality of it all, not just moving the mules, but seeing the people," Dr. Gonsoulin said. "It was just unreal, you know."

On another occasion, Dr. Gonsoulin and Dr. Sonny Corley, a LSU grad and veterinarian, stopped to rescue one simple mule. At least that was the idea. The problem was, a simple mule is an oxymoron of the highest proportions. The mule's owner had called the veterinary school days before, but the floodwaters had been too high in that area to do anything.

The owner of the mule was known throughout New Orleans as "the Candy Man." His mule pulled the famous "Taffy Wagon," throughout the French Quarter and around Jackson Square. The man didn't give rides; he simply sold candy to locals and tourists. And without his mule he was without a business.

When the waters finally began to recede, Dr. Corley and Dr. Gonsoulin, directions to the stable in hand, drove into the city in search of the Candy Man's mule. As the floodwaters were still relatively high, they had to park about three blocks away and slosh through the water to the old man's home.

"We walked up, and it was this old house with a carport," Dr. Gonsoulin recounted. "It had this twenty-foot garage, and the wind had pushed all this stuff against the doors, so we couldn't open them and go inside."

They were big, tall doors, made of corrugated tin. The two men managed to crack them enough to peek inside. There was no wall on the back of the garage. Peering through the crack they could see the Taffy Wagon, and near the wagon, in the back, they could see the mule still standing in his stall. Dr. Corley ventured around the barn to the back to get the mule, and Dr. Gonsoulin left to see whether he could get the truck and trailer any closer. After some time he returned, having brought the truck within a block of the house. As he walked back up to the house, Dr. Corley and the mule were nowhere to be found. Going closer to the garage, he heard a tremendous bang and a lot of metal-on-metal screeching and thrashing about. He stood for a moment not knowing what to do. He glanced down the street. He felt for his weapon, which was strapped to his hip. In that moment of confusion, the two large metal doors of the garage simply came loose and fell flat into the street amid a mountain of dust and debris, splashing down into the flooded roadway. There on the other side were Dr. Corley and the Candy Man's mule.

They called the owner as soon as they got back and let him know the mule had been caught. It didn't take long into the rescues to figure out that while rescued horses were "in our care," mules were simply "in custody."

Dr. Gonsoulin didn't hear much from the owner after that, but he read an article not long after the storms that the Candy Man was back in business. He was making do by pulling the Taffy Wagon with his truck, however, as he was keeping the mule at a friend's until he could get his house back in shape. Laughing to himself, Dr. Gonsoulin recalled, "It was great you know … isn't every day you get to say that you saved the Candy Man's mule."

Farther into the heart of New Orleans, another carriage stable awaited LSU's assistance. Throughout the wrath of the storm and the chaotic aftermath, Lucien Mitchell Jr. was carefully attending to the mules left in his charge. And come hell or high water, or both, Mitchell wasn't going anywhere until the mules could be safely evacuated as well.

Lucien Mitchell Sr. worked at the Charbonett Mid-City Carriage Stables, a company known for its touristy and romantic carriage rides throughout the French Quarter and downtown New Orleans. The younger Mitchell often helped out because he loved the horses and mules. When Katrina hit, Lucien Mitchell Jr. went to the stable to help his father and co-owner Darnell Stewart. Both Stewart and Mitchell Sr. were forced to evacuate, so when the floods came, Lucien Mitchell Jr. was the only person at the stables; with the torrential rains upon him, he decided he had no choice but simply to ride out the storm until help arrived.

At the height of the storm, Mitchell second-guessed staying put and tried to make a run for it. With more than a dozen horses and mules under his care, he decided that riding one horse, his favorite carriage horse, Fidel, and leading the rest of the herd might give him an opportunity to make it out of the city. Sloshing into the street, they made one futile attempt to escape a city already under siege from the storms.

"I was happy Fidel was there with me," Mitchell said. "We handled our business. He knew what the deal was, so he handled his business. I was real proud of 'im."

But the flooding was simply too much. With escape seeming highly improbable, Mitchell turned back. Deciding to wait it out, he took refuge with his animals in the battered stable, hoping that help would soon arrive.

Help would arrive, but not soon. In the darkness of the night, throughout the hellish days, his only comfort and his only conversation would be between him and the horses.

"Well, I was talkin' to 'em for a good while. For three days I was talkin' to 'em," he said.

While the horses were the very reason Mitchell stayed behind, they were also the reason he would eventually persevere. The company of animals carries a tremendous emotional lift. Whether it is a horse, or a dog, or a cat, having the companionship of another living thing is a powerful motivator. Just having the horses there with him, to stay busy looking after them, and even to talk to them throughout the day often helped keep the mood light in spite of the dreadful predicament that Mitchell faced.

"I was puttin' feed down and one of them [mules] picked it up and threw it," he said. "And I'm looking at this feed everywhere and was like 'you ain't gettin' no mo.' So he put his head down and was all sad looking, and I was like 'alright, you can have some more.' He didn't turn it over the second time."

With no electricity and little to eat, Mitchell continued to look after his herd. The hay and feed were getting low, and he realized he would have to do something soon. Hope of rescue came, but not in the form that Mitchell needed, or, rather, wanted. Rescuers arrived to get him out, but they had no way of getting the horses out.

"They kept saying 'c'mon man, we gonna rescue you' ... And I say, if you got a boat or a helicopter to rescue all these animals, then I'll go, and I'd just turn around and leave. Three or four times, I'd turned 'em down," he said.

Mitchell remained, but time was running out. "That's when hell started coming," Mitchell said. "I was all by myself ... and I was eating hot dogs out of a pack ... didn't realize I'd be staying eight days."

Eight days in the sweltering heat of New Orleans, in the worst conditions imaginable.

It may seem odd that someone would think so little of himself in a moment that might cause anyone to focus solely on self-preservation, but Lucien Mitchell knew each of these animals. He had seen some of them grow up. Strange as it may seem to some, these mules and draft horses were like family, and he wasn't about to walk out of the flooding and leave them behind.

Pointing to two mules in particular, he said, "they were raised together ... same as those," he said, pointing to another pair. "We bought 'em as a team. You might get away with like twenty minutes with one or the other out of the stall, but once one of them starts screaming and kicking for the other ... there's no way."

As he spent his days rationing out what little food remained for his animals and waiting for assistance, he could hear noise all around. Choppers flying by, people on boats yelling out, and still he waited.

"Day by day, it was like, man, I wish they'd come. I'd wonder do they know I'm here? Are they gonna come?" he said.

On day eight, help did arrive. Three LSU trucks and trailers rolled down the off ramp of Interstate 10, just north of Canal Street and parked at the head of Lafitte Street where the Mid-City Carriage Company was, and is still, located. Having learned of Mitchell's predicament and location from his father's telephone call, the crews came as quickly as access could be granted from both local authorities and floodwaters.

It was a miracle to Mitchell. The crews left their trucks and began to wade toward his barn. Lucien Mitchell Sr. was there as well, guiding the crews and wanting to be there to know whether his son had survived. The horses and mules were led through the waters to the roadway and transported to Lamar-Dixon, where Mitchell would again keep vigil by their sides and maintain watch over his herd until they could again return home.

Chapter 16

Rita

Just as we were getting a handle on things and really beginning to make some headway in New Orleans and the southern parishes that extend into the gulf, Hurricane Rita came ashore. She slammed into the Louisiana coast on September 23, causing additional flooding and bringing hurricane winds, rain, and fifteen-foot tidal surges into the southwestern regions of Louisiana.

The geography of this area is difficult to understand. Even twenty miles from Vermilion Bay off the Gulf of Mexico, shrimp boats are regularly docked in the marshes directly behind their owners' homes. It is a unique situation. Canals and waterways stretch inland from the bay for miles, making these waterways useful for boat travel and commerce. It makes for an interesting demographic. These are rural towns, where farming, ranching, and fishing are commonplace, and oil and gas are king.

While the actual storm was similar to Katrina, the aftermath was different in that the marshlands of southwestern Louisiana are not bounded by levees. The tidal surge swept seaward almost as quickly as it came ashore. Homes and businesses were ripped from their foundations, and shrimp boats and sea life were found miles from the shoreline in the middle of sugar cane fields. Most livestock were left in open pastures and fared very well, a lesson learned from Katrina.

Twenty-four hours before the storm hit, we reactivated our Horse Hurricane Helpline. A new staging area, the SugArena in New Iberia, Louisiana, was chosen as the most adequately and strategically located facility for housing displaced horses and other animals.

I drove to New Iberia the morning after the storm. Just north of the brunt of Rita's impact, the town was an ideal location to bring displaced animals, get them stabilized, and provide food, shelter, and medical care until the residents could decide what to do with them.

Dr. Gonsoulin, so instrumental in the rescues following Katrina, is actually from New Iberia. This was his stomping ground; these were his people, his neighbors and friends, and their animals. He seemed to know everyone and had a good sense for what was needed and what was not.

Dr. Gonsoulin had things already fairly organized at SugArena when I arrived. Two employees there handled the day-to-day operations, and they were well aware of the need for animal shelters following the storms.

SugArena is a large, open arena with a roof. There are a few rows of wooden stalls along the back and several pens for sorting hogs and sheep along the front corridor next to a small, enclosed office. It was basically designed as a local arena for 4-H shows, local rodeos, and equestrian events. Situated in the middle of a field in the heart of sugar cane country, the name was a given from the start.

Dr. Gonsoulin had contacted Terri Fitch, our friend from Lone Star Equine Rescue, and asked her to drive down from Lafayette to assist in coordinating the efforts, though it was unclear whether we would need the same type of assistance she and her husband, R.T., had so willingly provided for so many days following Katrina.

With the locals in charge and Terri Fitch having arrived to lend expertise from her experiences in Katrina, things were pretty well in hand at the shelter. A few animals had arrived, primarily dogs and cats, and were being housed in cages, with access to fans, feed, and water.

Dr. Phil DeVille, a local veterinarian from Abbeville, Louisiana, and I hopped into his truck and headed into Rita's wake to see how we could help. Having ridden together on a few missions during Katrina, we were both familiar with the routine. I had scribbled down a few notes from phone calls taken the night before. With so many individuals being sent in a hundred different directions over the past few weeks, we had forwarded the helpline number to a cellular phone I kept beside me at night.

The previous night three folks had called, wanting us to evacuate their animals. Rita's waters were quick. What had been merely rising waters were now flood areas nearly ten feet deep.

Chapter 16

As we drove along the back roads of Vermilion Parish, the devastation was evident. It was spotty though compared to Katrina's destruction. One road would be dry, the next would be wet, the next dry, and the next completely underwater. Operating from the ground, it was impossible to get a feel for the overall damage the area had received. Nothing made sense. Shrimp boats were seen miles from the coast. I saw a yellow-fin tuna in the middle of a field, flopping around in shallow water. Tuna don't live anywhere near the shoreline. This fish had come a long way.

Stopping at the first address, we were looking for a small herd of pygmy goats we had been told were living in a barn behind a house that backed up to a shrimp boat dock. The entire property was underwater. Goats are pretty resilient, however, and can climb nearly anything. I figured when the water got high, they would keep climbing whatever they could find. Quite honestly as I approached the house, I fully expected to see them on the roof. They were nowhere to be seen. A neighbor came from across the field to help us search. We waded in together, searching the waters, scouring the buildings, looking in trees and anywhere a goat might have sought refuge. It was eerie not knowing whether we were looking for live or dead animals. Our eyes went from all the locations where a live animal might have found a dry place to stand, to all of the dead zones where a carcass may have floated up and become lodged in debris or caught in a fence. And then there were alligators to be considered as well. If the goats hadn't found a dry foothold, there was little doubt they had either drowned or become victims of the local reptilian water patrol. We found nothing.

We moved on to our next destination. The call had come in early that morning. Twenty-three horses in Vermilion Parish needed to be moved due to impending floodwaters.

"Are the horses in a pasture or are they still in the barn?" I asked. "Both" was the reply. Vivid memories of horses locked in stalls consumed our minds. There were sure to be corpses.

As we drove down the never-ending parish country roads, we occasionally encountered the National Guard, usually just one-man operations at lonely intersections. "We are just out here to let everyone know they need to go slow and watch for wandering animals," the guard said. Then he sat back down on his chair in the middle of the road, machine gun at his side.

As we neared the address of the farm on our list, we saw only a few dead horses in the brush along the roadsides. We were beginning to take heart that most of the animals in Vermilion Parish had been left to roam in pastures, giving them a much better chance to swim and ultimately survive. The few that did succumb to the storm had simply become entangled in fences or debris and had been sucked down into the surge, and drowned. It was a devastating thing to witness, but we were encouraged that far fewer had met this end compared to entire barns that had been submerged during Katrina.

This was precisely our fear as we approached the farm where the horses had been left locked in their stalls. Driving through water, we reached the front gate and found a miracle. The water, as it moved north across the parish, had actually parted just yards before reaching the barn. Evidently the barn had been constructed in a location just high enough to avoid the flooding surge. The flooding went left and it went right, completely surrounding the barn like it was a tiny little island. Inside the horses were dry and alive. I couldn't believe their luck.

The homes in the area weren't so lucky. With the power and swiftness of the tidal surge, neighborhoods had simply been gutted. All the furniture and belongings inside had been pushed through doorways and broken windows and were now strewn across roadways and out into fields. Gas lines bubbled, and cars lay upside down everywhere. But the situation after Rita was different in that the water had receded very quickly. As fast as the surge had come, it had retreated to the ocean. Families, already back at home, dealt with the monumental task of recovering what was still useful and pushing the ruinous sludge through the front door and out into the yard. It was like landscaping in the family dining room. Mud and sludge a foot deep covered the first floor of almost every home we passed. Some of the homes still had a foot or more of water inside. As if the death of animals and the oddity of displaced sea life weren't enough, the reality of the devastating storm surge that came over the doorsteps into people's homes was like a slap in the face.

As the days progressed, the calls continued, and a rescue team was deployed to Sulphur, Louisiana. North of Lake Charles on the western side of Louisiana, Sulphur is practically in Texas. Rita had hit the town, and many evacuees had left their horses behind.

"Please go and get them," was the request, time after time.

First it was calling, then e-mailing. "I also have a few cows that I was wondering if you could get as well if you can get to them. The cows eat bread, so if you can take a loaf of bread you can coax them to you."

One crew returned after a day spent trying to rescue seventeen horses in the area. "It's impossible," the team reported, returning with only three of them. The horses were running loose in a field just off of an old country road. They were swamp horses, they were wild, and they had never seen a horse trailer in their lives.

Based on the e-mails we were receiving, it was difficult to tell exactly what the situation was going to look like when we arrived. A report from Dr. Sonny Corley informed us that the cows were doing fine and that the horses were all that needed to be evacuated. We knew the horses would need water, and we were bringing it with us in case we were unable to catch them and deliver them to SugArena.

I drove to Lamar-Dixon that evening and loaded up six empty fifty-gallon drums in the back of our LSU horse trailer. Back at the veterinary school, I filled each drum with water. It was nearly eleven. I was exhausted, and we were leaving for Sulphur at six the next morning. I parked my truck with the trailer in my yard, went inside, and fell asleep. The next thing I heard was a knock. Dr. Rusty Moore was at my door, and it was 6:30 a.m.

With two pickups full of staff, faculty, and volunteers from Lafayette, Louisiana, we headed west. Water is heavy, and the weight of the load was sucking gas a lot faster than I had anticipated. The closer we got to Sulphur, the more we realized fuel was going to be an issue. We were running low. No gas stations were open. Nothing. Everything had been abandoned. Finally, we spotted a station that appeared open and pulled in to purchase some gasoline.

The fuel station had been commandeered by the local law enforcement. Police cars sat by the pumps, and officers were running the register behind the counter inside.

"You can't refuel here," one of the officers said. "This fuel station is for emergency rescue operations only."

We explained our role, our mission that day, and our plight.

"I'm sorry," he said, "unless you have a federal fuel number, we can't give you any gasoline."

It was maddening. Here we had been carrying out rescue missions for weeks, and they wouldn't even sell us a tank of gas to get home on.

"Listen," I said, "I'm going to drive down this road and pick up seventeen horses that need to be evacuated and possibly treated for wounds from the storm. When I get them loaded, I am going to get back on the interstate and head for Baton Rouge. I am inevitably going to run out of gas and do you know what's going to happen then?

"I'm going to have to call the state patrol to come and help me, and they are going to have to go and get me some gasoline so that I can continue down the road, which is pretty ridiculous considering that governmental officials wouldn't allow me to buy any gas in the first place, don't you think?"

"I'm sorry," he said. "If you don't have a number, I can't sell you any gas."

We pushed on after the horses. There was nothing else we could do.

The volunteers that day included the entire LePoint family from Lafayette. Father, son, daughter, and wife, they had their own truck and a massive stock trailer, perfect for educating horses to the rules of the road. These were country folks, and every one of them could handle horses. The twelve-year-old son was as good with a horse as any grown man I've ever seen. He loved the stallions and assigned himself to their capture and care right from the beginning.

We caught them, slowly, cornering them and coaxing them with grain, until all were haltered and standing in line to be loaded into the horse trailer. The loading, however, would take nearly three hours. With the sheer number of horses to be crammed into two trailers, we needed to "stack" the horses sideways. Whether they collectively decided to oppose the operation, or whether each one had its own agenda, the problem with getting a thousand-pound animal to step up into a trailer, walk the length of the trailer, turn sideways, and stand nose to butt, butt to nose to maximize space, and then stay there in that position while we loaded the next one was not very high on any horse's agenda that day.

We pushed, we tugged, we coaxed with feed; nothing would work. We tried all the trailer-loading tricks in the book. We were patient, and we let them decide to load on their own. Nothing. We were impatient, and we gave them a little smack on the rear. Nothing. Then we did the only thing left to do. We lightly sedated them, plain and simple. With a few cc's of

Chapter *16*

sedative in their system, we basically used good old-fashioned "liquid rope" as Leslie Talley called it. The family of volunteers, Dr. Moore, Talley, and I lifted, pushed, and heaved seventeen masses of muscle into trailers and stacked them end to end. It was as frustrating a day as I ever had experienced, with or without a hurricane.

With the horses finally loaded, we set out for Lafayette on fumes. We tried the gas station again. No luck. But the officers were able to give us directions to a place where we could find fuel. We coasted in on our last drop. And then we waited an hour in line until we could get our $50 limit.

Onward we pushed down Interstate 10 East. And then the trailer started to sway back and forth. It banged and lurched, pushing the truck all over the road. We looked at each other; the sedatives were wearing off, and the horses were fighting. We pulled over on the interstate shoulder.

The horses had been so difficult to load, and so difficult to catch, that we had had little choice in the order in which we loaded them into the trailers. Ordinarily two stallions would have never been placed side by side, but given the circumstances, they were placed in whatever order we could manage.

Dr. Moore grabbed a syringe and a bottle of Detomidine (a sedative) and ran back to the trailer with traffic whizzing by. Reaching through the bars on the trailer, he sedated the horses once again to ensure that they wouldn't injure themselves during the long ride back to the shelter. Within seconds the stallions were calm again, and we continued down the road.

Then the brakes began to smoke. As we rolled into Lafayette, my truck was pouring smoke from every wheel.

"This isn't good," I said.

With no trailer brakes and the weight of a full load of horses, the brakes on the truck were fried. We pulled over again. As luck would have it, we were met by a local woman who knew just what we needed.

"Follow me," she said. "I know where there is a hose that works."

It may seem strange that a working hose would be such a precious commodity, but during the hurricanes of 2005, a working "anything" was rare indeed. We followed her down a back alley of Lafayette to a mobile Red Cross station. It was there — in the sweltering heat, crouching in the mud, covered in sweat, pouring water over the axles as steam rolled off the smoldering brake pads and as unruly horses banged away within the trailer — that smiles finally crept across our dirty faces.

Chapter **17**

Homecoming

"It's pure heart what you all are doing," one woman told me as we loaded up two miniature horses and an old pony named Nancy. Looking at the overall effort, she was probably right.

Heart is what got these horses out of these hurricane-ravaged areas. It was heart that drove any rescuer to do what he or she did. And it was heart that filled our volunteer lists, donated hay and feed, filled our supply rooms, bedded the stalls each night, brought us lunch and fresh water, and never asked for a thing in return.

Through the entire effort our greatest asset was our own perseverance, and the true heroes of the hurricane-relief effort were the countless volunteers. They would show up with their trucks and trailers to follow us into and through anything. They came prepared with ropes, halters, and tools. They worked tirelessly from sunup to sundown. They knew how to handle horses, and they did it all with good attitudes.

We weren't surprised to see so many volunteers arrive. The shocking thing was how many of them stayed. Rescuing horses from floods may seem glamorous. It isn't. It is dirty and grimy and sweaty and usually quite frustrating. And it takes ten times longer than anticipated to accomplish nearly anything. But the volunteers hung in there, and they made it happen. We had the logistics, the details; we had the plan. But without the volunteers, none of the happy endings would have been possible.

The process seemed never-ending, day in and day out hauling horses, rescuing dogs, and helping wherever we could. We kept some of the horses for weeks, looking after them, feeding and bandaging and tending to whatever needs they had. We treated them as if they were our own. We were determined to see it through to the end, whenever that was.

In addition to the sheer number of horses to care for at Lamar-Dixon, the heat and humidity, and the dwindling supply of equipment, there was also the added burden of human traffic in and out of the barns. Most of it was necessary and welcomed, but with more than a thousand human evacuees on the property and another thousand small-animal volunteers roaming around, no one could ever be sure who was who.

Unfortunately, the occasional visitor showed up, attempting to "buy" all of the horses from us. While volunteers often willingly offered to foster or adopt any horses that went unclaimed, several less-than-trustworthy characters offered to purchase or laid claim to a great number of the horses in our care. Bonnie Clark, the official coordinator of rescued horses at the Lamar-Dixon Expo Center, became very wary of these poseurs early in the

Chapter 17

game and took great measures to ensure every horse went back to its rightful owner. Each horse was identified with grease-pen markings. In addition, the horses were photographed, microchips were scanned and logged into a system, and daily check sheets were posted on each horse's stall, along with the name of the rightful owner.

When the National Guard took control of the safety of the area, Clark made them aware of the situation, and a security officer was assigned to each barn. Eventually, every individual on the grounds needed credentials. A small credentialing office was established, photographs were taken, and each individual with access to the area was logged into a database maintained by the National Guard.

As the days went by and the population of our herd increased, creating an accurate identification of each horse also became a crucial element in ensuring its well-being.

In Louisiana, microchips are the preferred means of permanent identification. These tiny chips, about the size of a grain of rice, are permanently embedded in the nuchal ligament of a horse's neck. An electronic radio frequency wand passed over the site will read the chip's identification number. This number not only identifies the horse but also corresponds to its Coggins test.

In Louisiana, every horse that travels to a horse show or to a racetrack, or traverses the state's highways for any reason, is required to have a Coggin's test. Developed by Dr. Leroy Coggins, this blood test determines whether a given horse is free from Equine Infectious Anemia virus (EIA). EIA is a viral disease that emerged in the United States in the late 1800s. It is transmitted to horses via the horsefly. There is neither a vaccine nor a cure. Although the disease can take up to a year to kill a horse, its symptoms — including fever, depression, loss of appetite, and a swollen belly and legs — are very debilitating and can be quite painful.

Although a positive case of EIA is rare, in 1993 Louisiana made regulatory history by taking the bold step of requiring permanent identification and annual EIA testing of all equines. Although Louisiana authorities estimate that fewer than 40 percent of the state's horses are tested annually, the public has responded favorably to the increased emphasis on EIA control.

When a Louisiana veterinarian performs a Coggins test on a horse for the first time, a microchip is also implanted that henceforth coincides with the horse's identification record. The vet then gives the owner a copy of the official record and sends a copy to the office of the state veterinarian so the registration is reported and stored.

With this in mind, Clark had every horse scanned with an electronic radio frequency wand. Any horse with a microchip was noted and the number was recorded. It seemed like a good route to take in positively identifying each horse on the premises and in verifying ownership.

The difficulty we encountered was two-fold: First, most of the rescued horses belonged to owners who had no way of transporting them and, therefore, had no official need for a Coggins test or a microchip. Second, when all of the identification numbers of horses with chips had been compiled, the list was sent

Chapter 17

to the Louisiana State Veterinarian's office in hopes the Coggins test records were in a database. This proved a huge frustration, as the state veterinarian's office had not finished compiling all the stored records electronically at that time. They are now digitally recorded and available, but during the aftermath of Hurricane Katrina, the agency simply had piles of paper Coggins test results and no way to use the numbers we provided them quickly and efficiently.

We were back at square one. With nearly four hundred horses in our possession, and very little to go by, we had to come up with a process to identify positively the true owner of each and every horse.

Fortunately, owners' calls informing us about each horse's whereabouts in the first place initiated most of the rescues. When we retrieved horses based on their information and brought them to Lamar-Dixon, we called the owners who would come and positively identify the horse or horses.

Other owners would come in search of their horses and simply describe them in detail before ever being allowed into the barn area. Occasionally, they had papers to prove ownership or pictures of the horse that helped us.

Happily, every horse in our care was ultimately claimed. Not one was ever shipped out of state nor given up to foster agencies. However, had we not been so fortunate in locating the true owner of each horse, we had a long list of volunteers waiting to adopt the horses in our care long. On the front of every stall, a makeshift "volunteer adoption list" could be seen with countless names that had asked to be contacted in the event the true owner could not be found. The offers of these foster homes were usually gestures made with the best intentions, but our goal was not to foster these animals; our goal was to get them home.

And then the owners came. Little by little, the owners of these equine hurricane survivors emerged. To witness the elation, the tearful reunions so long in the making, was a reward and a privilege.

Sharon Williams, whose Quarter Horse gelding Flash had been stabled at the Canal Street barn in St. Bernard Parish along with approximately forty other horses, called the Helpline several times. Dr. Ron Giardina had reported that this barn had taken the full force of the tidal surge and had been reduced from a large barn to a pile of rubble. Nine horses were found dead in the ruins, apparently the result of drowning. There were no signs of the remaining horses. This was reported to Williams, and while we had found several loose horses in the area, on levees and wandering through neighborhoods, it was doubtful that her beloved Flash had survived. "It doesn't look good," we told her, "but you are welcome to come to Lamar-Dixon and see if he is there."

On Saturday, September 10, Williams drove to Lamar-Dixon just to look through the barns on the off chance her horse had been rescued. A thirty-something woman, she combed the stalls and makeshift corrals in hopes that her eyes might lock on a familiar face. Dr. Rusty Moore was still at Lamar-Dixon that day after having sent several teams off on rescue missions. He walked with Williams for a while, trying to soothe her fears and console her. With so many horses being caught and rescued so far from their original homes, it was impossible to know whether a given horse had survived or perished until the owners came forward in search of their animals.

The two combed through stall after stall, walking down concrete corridors staring through metal railings at hundreds of different horses. All the while, Williams continued describing her horse, giving detailed accounts of his color and markings. They searched each barn for Flash; Williams hopefully gazing with anticipation down each shed row and quickly examining every pair of eyes and every swish of tail or twitch of ears from the horse inside a stall. Dr. Moore continued along with her, silently hoping they would find something as well, yet dreading that awful moment when they came to the last stall.

It is odd to search for a lost horse with its owner. So many times over countless days and hours, we had trudged through streets and neighborhoods in search of missing horses. But they weren't our horses, and their rightful owners weren't usually at our side. It was different when the owners finally arrived. We felt responsible. We tried everything we knew to locate the animals in question; it was almost as if we felt that our work was now being judged by whether a horse had made it into our care.

In that moment when Dr. Moore was searching for the right thing to say, and Williams had exhausted every story of her horse she could think of, the pair happened upon Flash. He stood alone in his stall and came forward as Dr. Moore unlatched the door. Williams hustled inside, laughing and crying. She said very little, hugging him quietly for a long time.

"Thank you so much," was all she could manage.

It was more than enough.

I remember Dr. Ashley Stokes saying, "When you see the help-lessness that people have felt, not being able to go back in to these flooded areas ... the stress of not knowing ... when we're able to help, it really meant the world to them."

We had made a difference. Probably in ways we'll never really know. Darren Rogers Jr., a young boy whose horse, Shine, was stabled at a barn in New Orleans East, came by Lamar-Dixon the same day that Sharon found Flash. He and his father had walked through all three barns of rescued horses. Shine wasn't there. A heartbroken boy and a helpless-feeling father walked slowly across the parking lot. "Shine is gone forever," they acknowledged.

As they shuffled toward their car scanning the barns one last time in the blazing afternoon heat, Dr. Moore noticed them and inquired about their horse. After a short visit he said, "There are still a few horses in makeshift corrals in the main arena ... have you looked over there?"

They raced to the arena. In the shaded main arena of Lamar-Dixon, several makeshift corrals had been thrown together. Some were private areas for stallions that would not behave well next to other horses. Others were for small herds of horses found together. It was a smorgasbord of horses, with equines of every size and shape making up the various little bands; large horses, ponies, miniatures, old and young and of every color imaginable. The boy scanned each herd. He ran down the dusty rows between the corrals examining every horse, calling out for Shine. It was heartbreaking given the fear that Shine might not be among the herd. As the youngster called out yet again, a black horse turned. In a second the boy was through the arena fence railing and dashing across the dirt floor. Shine looked up, and if a horse could have swept that kid up, this one would have been there with open arms.

Confusion, chaos, days of searching on end through more devastation than any of us had ever seen, thousands of dollars in fuel, and nights with little sleep. These things didn't seem to matter much when we saw things come full circle.

As joyous as it was to see these reunions, we also lived daily with the grief of so many individuals who held out hope for weeks, only to learn that their animals were never found.

In the days following Hurricane Rita, Dr. Dan Burba, Leslie Talley, and I took a reconnaissance flight over lower Plaquemines Parish with the help of a helicopter and crew from the U.S. Coast Guard. It became clear that rebuilding Louisiana would take years. Looking down on the devastation brought on by Katrina and worsened by Rita, it was surprising that anything had survived at all. Little was left to be done from a rescue standpoint. Those that needed to be rescued had been; those that could manage on their own were left behind. And as the waters receded and the rebuilding efforts ensued, one by one horses left our care to return to their owners.

It is impossible to recount every story and every occasion we experienced. This story is told from my perspective and through many discussions and interviews with the people who

Appendix

Emergency Preparedness Guide for Horse Owners

What would you do if you knew with absolute certainty that a catastrophic natural disaster would definitely strike your home or farm and that you had five days to prepare? What if you had five hours? What if you had five *minutes*?

The stories of equine rescues from the aftermath of Hurricane Katrina (and Rita) in *Horses of the Storm* are shared for a number of reasons. The primary purpose is to make horse owners aware of the harsh realities that many had to face so that we can learn from their experiences and benefit from the knowledge we now have.

It is important that these stories be recorded, and I think it is also important to detail the lessons learned, so that we will be better prepared to ensure the well-being of our animals both during and prior to the next hurricane, wildfire, flood, or other disaster.

WHAT WE LEARNED

During the horse rescues of Katrina, we learned our lessons on the go; we had no choice. But for our own future endeavors, and for communities around the nation, there is an opportunity now to learn from our mistakes and from our successes.

1) Dedication

Dedication was the priceless #1 on every list of the things we learned about horse rescues, or any rescue efforts for that matter. The mistakes we made were plentiful, but our ambition to see the effort through and our willingness to correct our mistakes to continue our work were evident throughout the process. Dedication is the foundation of any success.

2) Coordination

We learned that coordinating rescue activities is paramount. Not only do all members of a team need to be aware of all aspects of the effort, but coordinating efforts through a state or federal agency is necessary. In the United States, the National Incident Management System (NIMS) is technically in charge of recovery for every type of major natural or manmade disaster. The Incident Command System within NIMS is the ultimate decision maker in all regards to rescue efforts. We didn't know that when we started; we learned it as we went along. Not only did following established protocol prove to be the correct thing to do, it was also a huge step forward in gaining access to additional search areas, personnel, and much needed equipment and supplies.

3) Flexibility

We learned to be flexible and to realize that a disaster situation is exactly that. It is a disaster when it occurs and it is a disaster to try to recover. It is a trying time in terms of physical exhaustion, communication, and logistics. It is hard and the emotional toll is almost unbearable, but "going with the flow" helps keep things in perspective and puts focus on the higher purpose of what is being done; providing assistance to those in need.

4) Staying Positive

My father once told me that to be happy in life, the important thing to remember is to stay positive and stay busy. Those wise words never proved to be as valuable as during the rescue days following Katrina. Staying busy was easy. Staying positive was a challenge, and the ability to roll with the punches, to keep the higher good in mind and to keep moving forward was a challenge for everyone on any level of the rescue effort. But it works.

5) Being Prepared

"Be Prepared" is the simple Boy Scout motto, yet it is so easy to forget until it is too late. The problem is you never know when "too late" is going to come. You may have a week-long warning; you may have ten minutes. Preparation and the ability to respond actively with a plan are absolutely crucial to surviving any disaster. It is also your animal's best defense as well. We have to plan for them, keep them in mind in our evacuation or disaster response plans, not only on the federal and state levels, but as individuals. Be aware of your animals when you consider the potential emergencies that could happen. Where will they go and how will they get there? These are among your responsibilities as an animal owner, and you owe it to yourself and your animals to have a plan.

HOW TO BE PREPARED

The types of disasters vary so widely that there is no single all-encompassing plan on which we can accurately depend for every situation. We must prepare for anything that could possibly occur that may affect our homes, our property, our animals, and even our lives. Knowing how you would respond, the exact actions you would take, the supplies and equipment you would need, the escape routes, methods of communication, and the necessary contacts you will need are critical elements of a successful plan. When you have an answer that you fully trust for each of the three scenarios described previously—five days warning; five hours warning; five minutes warning—you are most likely well prepared.

If you are evacuating your home or your farm, if at all possible, take your horses with you. If you cannot take them with you, take measures to ensure that they have the greatest opportunity to survive whatever impending disaster is headed your way. Place identification on your horses so that they can be reunited with you if they become lost. This can be done in any number of ways and is addressed in detail later in this section. Use any method you can think of that will possibly reunite you with your horses. It will be heart-wrenching to leave them, and it will cause you days and possibly weeks of worry and wonder, but it can work if you have no other option. Remember, options are what you want, and options are what you will have if you are prepared.

Communities nationwide also need to have a formal disaster response plan that includes consideration for animal management. To do this, state and regional jurisdictions need simply to become familiar with what is known as the National Response Plan. Training and credentialing workshops are available nationwide for individuals interested in learning to be a team member of a certified rescue effort. Leadership at state and regional levels needs to develop specific processes to help train and educate the massive volunteer efforts that this country is so good at developing. Find out if your community is prepared. If it's not, consider what you can do to encourage your community to get with the program. Maybe the leader that's needed is you.

For those organizing emergency response activities, volunteers can get you through the most difficult times with extra hands, extra vehicles, and much needed supplies. To be able to bring a glimmer of hope and success to a catastrophic situation is a very contagious thing. Volunteers will drive nonstop for days and nights to come to your aid if they truly believe they can help. They *can* help, but they need guidance in order to be as effective as possible. They are vital to any rescue effort, but they need to be trained to know what to do, how to do it, and when to do it. It is the responsibility of state and community planning agencies both to understand that volunteer training is needed and to deliver it.

READINESS QUIZ

First, assess your current situation and see where you stand in regard to being truly prepared. Start by asking yourself a few basic questions to see how you currently measure up — be brutally honest.

❏ **Yes**   ❏ **No**   I have a written emergency plan for my animals.

❏ **Yes**   ❏ **No**   My emergency plan has options for different types of emergencies and differing time periods of advanced warning.

❏ **Yes**   ❏ **No**   I have a backup plan for my animals in the event that I am out of town when a disaster strikes.

❏ **Yes**   ❏ **No**   *All* of my horses can be loaded into a trailer quickly and calmly.

❏ **Yes**   ❏ **No**   I own or have access to the necessary truck, trailer, and driver for all of my horses to be transported out of the area quickly and safely.

❏ **Yes**   ❏ **No**   The truck and trailer used to haul my horses are in good working order, and I maintain an adequate supply of fuel for any type of evacuation.

❏ **Yes**   ❏ **No**   I can quickly equip all of my horses with breakaway halters and identification tags.

❏ **Yes**   ❏ **No**   I have photos of my horses, as well as other proof-of-ownership identification.

❏ **Yes**   ❏ **No**   My horses are vaccinated and up-to-date on Coggins and health papers. The vaccinations include tetanus.

❏ **Yes**   ❏ **No**   Copies of these vaccinations and negative Coggins reports are stored in my emergency kit.

❏ **Yes**   ❏ **No**   I know where I will go in the event of an emergency, and I have evacuation maps.

❏ **Yes**   ❏ **No**   I have given a copy of my plan and contact information to a friend based far away from me.

❏ **Yes**   ❏ **No**   I have a cell phone and the means to keep it fully charged.

❏ **Yes**   ❏ **No**   I have put together an evacuation kit with supplies, water, and feed for three days for my horses.

❏ **Yes**   ❏ **No**   If I cannot take all my horses, I have prioritized the ones to take and have something to mark identification on the others.

How many "Yes" responses did you check? How many "No" responses?

Analyzing these simple questions will give you a good starting point on how you need to move forward in order to be adequately prepared for a catastrophic situation. If there are any areas you feel you need to improve or address, make it a priority to do so soon while time and the resources to prepare are abundant.

YOUR HORSES ARE *YOUR* RESPONSIBILITY

Federal, state, and local organizations have countless resources and guidelines available that will assist you in your planning. But remember — federal, state, and local authorities are only there to *assist* us; they are *not* responsible for *your* decisions. And while help may ultimately arrive in your time of need, the chief responsibility for survival is your own. Carefully formulate a plan now, while there is time, which will give you your best chance for a successful outcome.

❖ First, take the responsibility of being a horse owner seriously and prepare for any type of natural or manmade disaster well ahead of time.

❖ Take the time to ponder the possible catastrophes that could feasibly occur in your area and to consider your options seriously. You don't have to sit around waiting for the sky to fall, but think about what has historically occurred in your area, be it earthquakes, hurricanes, tornadoes, wildfires, flooding—whatever.

❖ Prepare a solid plan of action to respond to these occurrences in the most effective manner.

❖ Consider what you'll need, and how you will carry out your evacuation plan, or your emergency plan.

❖ Most important, make time to do it *now* while you have the resources all around you to prepare and the incredible luxury of time to get things well organized.

Appendix

■ *Vaccinations*

An emergency situation may be a time when your horse could potentially be exposed to many other horses. This can be a dangerous time for your horse in terms of communicable diseases and you want to ensure that all preventative vaccines have been administered to protect your horse's health.

> ❖ All horses should have current vaccinations for tetanus and encephalitis viruses (Eastern, Western, and West Nile).
>
> ❖ Test for EIA and keep a record of a current negative Coggins test for all of your horses. This will verify that your horses are free of Equine Infectious Anemia and thereby legal to transport down state highways and across state lines.
>
> ❖ Keep copies of your horse's current vaccination record and Coggins test in your trailer, in your emergency kit, in your personal papers — wherever you think it's necessary.

■ *Identification*

Your horse should have two forms of identification: a permanent form, such as a microchip, brand, or tattoo, and a temporary one that you can attach to the horse immediately prior to an impending emergency. Temporary identification should serve as a back-up means of identification and should include basic information about the horse and contact information about the owner. Simply include your name, your home address, e-mail address, and any telephone numbers where you can be reached.

You may also want to include your horse's name, breed, and age; however, the greatest importance of these forms of identification is to link the animal with a rightful owner. The issue of determining a horse's age, sex, and breed can be easily accomplished. Determining who owns the horse is another matter. This is the problem you want to avoid, and multiple forms of identification will help minimize the lack of information.

❖ Microchip identification. Even if your state does not require this, do it anyway. Register your microchip with your state veterinarian's office via your primary veterinarian. Also, keep backup records of your horse's microchip number.

❖ Freeze branding. If you are unfamiliar with freeze branding, talk to your veterinarian. Not only can your veterinarian show you how to freeze brand your horse, but he or she can also give you information about branding in your state, such as registration.

❖ Tattoos – used primarily for racehorses, lip tattoos are another way to identify your horses permanently.

❖ Keep photographs of your horse (with you) and a general description of your horse's color and markings that will help both to identify your horse and establish ownership. You may even want to keep a copy of this information with a number of friends in the event that your own home is destroyed.

❖ One means of a temporary form of identification is a luggage tag with your horse's information and your personal contact information. This luggage tag can then be fastened onto your horse's halter and/or braided into your horse's mane or tail. Luggage tags are not expensive, so have several on hand in case you need additional temporary ID tags (if you have to board at a shelter, for example).

❖ Alternatively, you can write your name and telephone number on your horse's coat with greasepaint or a livestock crayon. You can even use spray paint if you have no other option.

❖ Using indelible ink, write your name and contact information on duct tape and tape it to your horse.

❖ Another very good form of temporary identification is the use of a wax paper wristband similar to what you might receive if you attend a concert or special event. Record your horse's information and your personal contact information in permanent marker onto a regular wax paper wristband and place it around the pastern or fetlock of your horse. These wristbands can survive nearly any type of weather, they last a very long time, they are strong and do not easily become caught on debris. However, should they become caught on anything during a disaster, they will ultimately break away.

■ *Share Information*

❖ What good is all of your planning if nobody else knows about it? Tell your friends, your neighbors, and your relatives of your plans and keep them abreast of your actions during times of emergency.

❖ Network a plan with area neighbors who also have horses. Share emergency and evacuation plans. You will be sharing life-saving information and may be able to implement new ideas into your own plan. Shared information is vital to a successful community response to a given situation.

■ *Know Your Local Authorities*

❖ Become familiar with your state and local authorities and their recommendations for emergency response for animal owners. Most states and county/parish officials have plans in place. These plans are much more effective if the citizens of the area are actually informed of the plan, understand the particulars, are aware of the resources available, and are prepared to respond in an organized fashion.

❖ Be aware of emergency phone numbers and contacts that can assist you from your local law enforcement, your veterinarian, and your county/parish Emergency Operations Center.

■ *Evacuation Plans*

❖ Develop a solid evacuation plan.

❖ First, identify the equipment that will be used (trucks and trailers) and maintain them in good working order so that your situation is not compromised by a mechanical failure.

❖ Equipment also includes communication devices (cell phones, satellite phones) that will be used during the trip to maintain contact with those that can assist you should you experience difficulty during travel.

❖ Second, identify the destination you will travel to in situations that require evacuation. This can be a neighbor's farm, a distant relative or friend, or an equine facility that you have made arrangements with that is well out of the path of danger. Make arrangements now so that you aren't caught scrambling at the last minute.

❖ Third, identify your route and possible alternate routes that will be used during evacuation that will allow for your safe and timely passage out of the area of danger. If you have advance warning, and if at all possible, plan to leave at least 72 hours before an impending disaster. Clearly, this is not often possible, but always take advantage of your greatest ally — time.

❖ Fourth, make sure your friends and family are aware of your evacuation plans and the routes you will travel.

■ *First-Aid Kits*

Prepare an emergency first-aid kit that can be easily transported. This kit should include:

- ❖ Any medications your horse is currently taking
- ❖ Medications that may be needed
- ❖ Any syringes or needles required to administer medication
- ❖ Ointments for wounds
- ❖ Hydrogen peroxide
- ❖ Bandages and wraps
- ❖ Medical towels
- ❖ Scissors
- ❖ Medical tape
- ❖ Two thermometers
- ❖ Flashlight (with fresh batteries)
- ❖ Hoof knife
- ❖ Sterile gauze pads
- ❖ Vetwrap
- ❖ Additional halters and lead ropes
- ❖ Cotton-tipped swabs
- ❖ Hand-sanitizing towels
- ❖ Eye flush
- ❖ Insect repellent
- ❖ Furazone
- ❖ Blue Kote spray
- ❖ Horseman's Dream Cream
- ❖ And any items you would typically have on hand that would be needed for minor physical ailments

or conditions. There are basics that you will need, but every horse is unique and will require attention in this regard.

❖ REMEMBER: Prepare *your* kit for *your* horse.

■ *Food and Water*

❖ Horses are creatures of habit and routine. Upset the routine and you'll upset the horse. Be prepared to have your horse's usual diet available so that you can maintain regular feedings with the feed to which your horse is accustomed.

■ *Preparing To Weather the Storm*

❖ There may be an occasion when "riding out the storm" is the only alternative. Being consigned to this predicament does not mean that your situation is hopeless. Never consider that you are simply at the mercy of a storm or catastrophic situation. A plan for a five-minute response can be just as important and effective as a plan for a five-day response, provided that you maintain your focus and carry out your pre-determined course of action.

❖ Prepare your property to receive the blow. Remove any debris to prevent unnecessary damage that can be caused by high winds or fires.

❖ Decide whether to keep your horses inside a barn or in an open field. Your choice in this matter should depend on the situation. If you face a wildfire or flooding, a barn is not a safe place. If you are preparing for hail and a thunderstorm, a barn may indeed be the safest place. The situation will determine how you should respond; however, you need to make the choice that you will apply to a given situation now during your planning phase to avoid bad judgments and hasty responses in the midst of a crisis.

❖ In some cases, depending on your situation, it can be necessary for you simply to set your horse free. It is possible that there will be no pasture where a horse can be safely placed. If you find that you have no means to transport your horse to safety, and your best judgment indicates that locking the horse inside a barn or stall would not be in the best interest of the animal, simply leading the horse outside and turning it loose may be the best option. However, this should be a *last-resort* option, one that should only be employed under the direst of circumstances. Consider the landscape of where you are located and the possible escape routes your horse may take during the disaster. An escape from a thunderstorm onto a busy interstate is *not* a good option. An escape from a potential tornado into a national forest may be a good option. Always use your best judgment; your horse's life depends on it. Animals have an incredible survival instinct. They may end up miles from your home, but their chances of survival are exponentially increased if they are given the opportunity to flee under their own power. Provided the proper identification methods have been employed, it is highly likely that you will be reunited with your horse.

❖ Consider the structure of your barn and the refuge or danger that it might present. Keep the aisles free from unnecessary debris. If you are turning horses out into the pasture, be mindful of the potential for flying debris, falling power lines or trees, etc.

❖ Halter *every* horse. Only use halters that will break in the event that they become entangled — do *not* use nylon halters. Halters can be valuable in identifying a horse, allow identification materials to be attached, and are highly useful in catching and handling stranded horses and leading them to safety.

❖ Keep at least a two- to three-week supply of hay, grain, and water in a storm-proof container. Wrap hay in plastic or waterproof tarps and store it well above the ground floor. Fill all stock tanks with water. Additional water may be stored in large plastic containers (trash cans). Maintain an emergency barn kit, which should include equipment for clean-up and repair, i.e., a chainsaw, hammer, saw, nails, screws, wire, pliers, and other fencing materials.

❖ Store an ample supply of flashlights and batteries, or lanterns with the necessary fuel. Also, keep a portable radio with fresh batteries so that you can still get information in the event of a power loss.

Every emergency is unique, and provided that you have ample warning, the most assured measure of successfully surviving is to evacuate the area. Beyond that, there are countless measures you can employ to increase the chance for a successful outcome but you must have a plan.

Time is a precious commodity in so many regards but particularly when responding to the effects of a disaster or the warning of a potential disaster. It is all too common for any of us to take things for granted when all is going well. But if any wisdom has been gleaned from the destruction and loss of life brought on by Hurricane Katrina, it is that we cannot take Mother Nature for granted. We must anticipate that the worst possible scenario can occur and understand that the sole responsibility for preparing for our own survival, that of our loved ones, and of our animals is in fact, our own.

RESOURCES

National Agency Contact Information

Many of these organizations provide valuable information and resource tools to prepare yourself, your family, pets, home, business, and property for an emergency. Visit their Web sites to learn more.

American Association of Equine Practitioners

www.aaep.org

American Red Cross

www.redcross.org

American Society for the Prevention of Cruelty to Animals

www.aspca.org

American Veterinary Medical Foundation

www.avma.org

Centers for Disease Control & Prevention

www.cdc.gov

Emergency Animal Rescue Service (EARS) [part of United Animal Nations group]

www.uan.org

EquineU.com

www.equineu.com

FEMA (Federal Emergency Management Association)

www.fema.gov

Humane Society of the United States (HSUS)

www.hsus.org.

National Flood Insurance Program

www.floodsmart.gov

National Weather Service

www.nws.noaa.gov

Occupational Safety & Health Administration

www.osha.gov

Ready Business

www.ready.gov

Small Business Administration

www.sba.gov

Social Security Administration

www.ssa.gov

United States Equestrian Federation (USEF)

www.usef.org

Appendix

EMERGENCY PHONE NUMBERS

FIRE DEPARTMENT AND EMERGENCY _____ **911**

SHERIFF'S DEPARTMENT _____

NON-EMERGENCY _____

ASPCA ANIMAL POISON CONTROL _____

ANIMAL CONTROL_____

AGRICULTURAL EXTENSION OFFICE _____

OTHER IMPORTANT NUMBERS _____

_____

_____

_____

_____

PERSONAL PHONE NUMBERS

DOCTOR _____

FAMILY _____

NEIGHBOR _____

NEIGHBOR _____

VETERINARIAN_____

VETERINARIAN_____

FARRIER _____

OTHER PERSONAL NUMBERS _____

_____

_____

_____

MY HORSE

HORSE'S NAME _____

BREED _____

COLOR / MARKINGS _____

GENDER _____

YEAR FOALED / APPROXIMATE AGE _____

DATE OF PHOTO _____

AFFIX PHOTO OF HORSE HERE

MY HORSE

HORSE'S NAME _____

BREED _____

COLOR / MARKINGS _____

GENDER _____

YEAR FOALED / APPROXIMATE AGE _____

DATE OF PHOTO _____

AFFIX PHOTO OF HORSE HERE

Offices and Agencies of Emergency Management

www.usa.gov
www.dhs.gov

FEMA
500 C St. SW
Washington, D.C. 20472
Disaster Assistance: (800) 621-FEMA
TTY (800) 462-7585 www.fema.gov

Alabama Emergency Management Agency
5898 County Road 41
PO Drawer 2160
Clanton, AL 35046-2160
(205) 280-2200
(205) 280-2495 FAX
ema.alabama.gov/

Alaska Division of Homeland Security and Emergency Management
PO Box 5750
Fort Richardson, AK 99505-5750
(907) 428-7000
(907) 428-7009 FAX
www.ak-prepared.com

American Samoa Territorial Emergency Management
Coordination (TEMCO)

American Samoa Government
PO Box 1086
Pago Pago, American Samoa 96799
(011) (684) 699-6415
(011) (684) 699-6414 FAX

Arizona Division of Emergency Management
5636 E. McDowell Road
Phoenix, AZ 85008
(602) 244-0504
(800) 411-2336
www.azdema.gov

Arkansas Department of Emergency Management
Bldg. # 9501 Camp Joseph T. Robinson
North Little Rock, AR 72199-9600
(501) 683-6700
(501) 683-7890 FAX
www.adem.arkansas.gov/

California Governor's Office of Emergency Services
3650 Schriever Ave.
Mather, CA 95655-4203
(916) 845-8510
(916) 845-8511 FAX
www.oes.ca.gov/

Colorado Office of Emergency Management
Division of Local Government
Department of Local Affairs
9195 E. Mineral Ave., Suite 200
Centennial, CO 80112
(720) 852-6600
(720) 852-6750 Fax
www.dola.state.co.us/oem/oemindex.htm

Connecticut Office of Emergency Management
Department of Emergency Management and Homeland
Security
360 Broad St.
Hartford, CT 06105
(860) 566-3180
(860) 247-0664 FAX
www.ct.gov/demhs/site/default.asp

Delaware Emergency Management Agency
165 Brick Store Landing Road
Smyrna, DE 19977
(302) 659-3362
(302) 659-6855 FAX
www.state.de.us/dema/index.htm

District of Columbia Emergency Management Agency
2720 Martin Luther King, Jr. Ave., S.E.
Second Floor
Washington, D.C. 20032
(202) 727-6161
(202) 673-2290 FAX
dcema.dc.gov

Florida Division of Emergency Management
2555 Shumard Oak Blvd.
Tallahassee, FL 32399-2100
(850) 413-9969
(850) 488-1016 FAX
floridadisaster.org

Georgia Emergency Management Agency
PO Box 18055
Atlanta, GA 30316-0055
(404) 635-7000
(404) 635-7205 FAX
www.State.Ga.US/GEMA/

Office of Civil Defense, Government of Guam
PO Box 2877
Hagatna, Guam 96932
(011) (671) 475-9600
(011) (671) 477-3727 FAX
http://ns.gov.gu/

Guam Homeland Security/Office of Civil Defense
221B Chalan Palasyo
Agana Heights, Guam 96910
(671) 475-9600
(671) 477-3727 FAX
www.guamhs.org

Hawaii State Civil Defense
3949 Diamond Head Road
Honolulu, HI 96816-4495
(808) 733-4300
(808) 733-4287 FAX
www.scd.hawaii.gov

Idaho Bureau of Homeland Security
4040 Guard St., Bldg. 600
Boise, ID 83705-5004

(208) 422-3040
(208) 422-3044 FAX
www.bhs.idaho.gov/

Illinois Emergency Management Agency
2200 S. Dirksen Pkwy.
Springfield, IL 62703
(217) 782-2700
(217) 524-7967 FAX
www.state.il.us/iema

Indiana Department of Homeland Security
Indiana Government Center South
302 W. Washington St., Room E208
Indianapolis, IN 46204-2767
(317) 232-3986
(317) 232-3895 FAX
www.ai.org/sema/index.html

Indiana State Emergency Management Agency
302 W. Washington St.
Room E-208 A
Indianapolis, IN 46204-2767
(317) 232-3986
(317) 232-3895 FAX
www.ai.org/sema/index.html

Iowa Homeland Security & Emergency Management
Division
Department of Public Defense
Hoover Office Bldg.
Des Moines, IA 50319
(515) 281-3231
(515) 281-7539 FAX
Iowahomelandsecurity.org.

Kansas Division of Emergency Management
2800 S.W. Topeka Blvd.
Topeka, KS 66611-1287
(785) 274-1401
(785) 274-1426 FAX
www.ink.org/public/kdem/

Kentucky Emergency Management
EOC Bldg.
100 Minuteman Pkwy., Bldg. 100
Frankfort, KY 40601-6168
(502) 607-1682
(502) 607-1614 FAX
kyem.ky.gov/

Louisiana Office of Emergency Preparedness
7667 Independence Blvd.
Baton Rouge, LA 70806
(225) 925-7500
(225) 925-7501 FAX
www.ohsep.louisiana.gov

Maine Emergency Management Agency
45 Commerce Drive, Suite #2
#72 State House Station
Augusta, ME 04333-0072
207-624-4400
207-287-3180 (FAX)
www.state.me.us/mema/memahome.htm

Homeland Security and Emergency Management Division
Michigan Department of State Police
Michigan State Police
4000 Collins Road
Lansing, MI 48910
(517) 333-5042
(517) 333-4987 FAX
www.michigan.gov/emd

CNMI Emergency Management Office
Office of the Governor
Commonwealth of the Northern Mariana Islands
PO Box 10007
Saipan, Mariana Islands 96950
(670) 322-9529
(670) 322-7743 FAX
www.cnmiemo.gov.mp

National Disaster Management Office
Office of the Chief Secretary
PO Box 15
Majuro, Republic of the Marshall Islands 96960-0015
(011) (692) 625-5181
(011) (692) 625-6896 FAX

Maryland Emergency Management Agency
Camp Fretterd Military Reservation
5401 Rue Saint Lo Drive
Reistertown, MD 21136
(410) 517-3600
(877) 636-2872 Toll-Free
(410) 517-3610 FAX
www.mema.state.md.us/

Massachusetts Emergency Management Agency
400 Worcester Road
Framingham, MA 01702-5399
(508) 820-2000
(508) 820-2030 FAX
www.state.ma.us/mema

Michigan Division of Emergency Management
4000 Collins Road
PO Box 30636
Lansing, MI 48909-8136
(517) 333-5042
(517) 333-4987 FAX
www.michigan.gov/msp/1,1607,7-123-1593_3507---,00.html

National Disaster Control Officer
Federated States of Micronesia
PO Box PS-53
Kolonia, Pohnpei - Micronesia 96941
(011) (691) 320-8815
(001) (691) 320-2785 FAX

Minnesota Homeland Security and Emergency
Management Division,
Minnesota Department of Public Safety
444 Cedar St., Suite 223
St. Paul, MN 55101-6223
(651) 296-0466
(651) 296-0459 FAX
www.hsem.state.mn.us

Mississippi Emergency Management Agency
PO Box 5644
Pearl, MS 39288-5644
(601) 933-6362, (800) 442-6362
(601) 933-6800 FAX
www.msema.org www.msema.org/mitigate/mssaferoominit.htm

Missouri Emergency Management Agency
PO Box 116
2302 Militia Drive
Jefferson City, MO 65102
(573) 526-9100
(573) 634-7966 FAX
sema.dps.mo.gov

Montana Division of Disaster & Emergency Services
1900 Williams St.
Helena, MT 59604-4789
(406) 841-3911
(406) 444-3965 FAX
dma.mt.gov/des/

Nebraska Emergency Management Agency
1300 Military Road
Lincoln, NE 68508-1090
(402) 471-7410
(402) 471-7433 FAX
www.nema.ne.gov

Nevada Division of Emergency Management
2525 S. Carson St.
Carson City, NV 89711
(775) 687-4240
(775) 687-6788 FAX
dem.state.nv.us/

Governor's Office of Emergency Management
State Office Park South
107 Pleasant St.
Concord, NH 03301
(603) 271-2231; (603) 225-7341 FAX
www.nhoem.state.nh.us/

New Jersey Office of Emergency Management
Emergency Management Bureau
PO Box 7068
West Trenton, NJ 08628-0068
(609) 538-6050 Monday-Friday
(609) 882-2000 ext. 6311 (24/7)
(609) 538-0345 FAX
www.state.nj.us/oem/county/

New Mexico Department of Public Safety
Office of Emergency Management
PO Box 1628
13 Bataan Blvd.
Santa Fe, NM 87505
(505) 476-9600
(505) 476-9635 Emergency
(505) 476-9695 FAX
www.dps.nm.org/emergency/index.htm

Emergency Management Bureau
Department of Public Safety
PO Box 1628
13 Bataan Blvd.
Santa Fe, NM 87505
(505) 476-9606
(505) 476-9650
www.dps.nm.org/emc.htm

New York State Emergency Management Office
1220 Washington Ave.
Bldg. 22, Suite 101
Albany, NY 12226-2251
(518) 292-2275
(518) 457-9995 FAX
www.nysemo.state.ny.us/

North Carolina Division of Emergency Management
4713 Mail Service Center
Raleigh, NC 27699-4713
(919) 733-3867
(919) 733-5406 FAX
www.dem.dcc.state.nc.us/

North Dakota Department of Emergency Services
PO Box 5511
Bismarck, ND 58506-5511
(701) 328-8100
(701) 328-8181 FAX
www.nd.gov/des

Ohio Emergency Management Agency
2855 W. Dublin-Granville Road
Columbus, OH 43235-2206
(614) 889-7150
(614) 889-7183 FAX
ema.ohio.gov/ema.asp

Office of Civil Emergency Management
Will Rogers Sequoia Tunnel
2401 N. Lincoln
Oklahoma City, OK 73152
(405) 521-2481
(405) 521-4053 FAX
www.odcem.state.ok.us/

Oregon Emergency Management
Department of State Police
PO Box 14370
Salem, OR 97309-5062
(503) 378-2911; (503) 373-7833 FAX
egov.oregon.gov/OOHS/OEM

Palau NEMO Coordinator, Office of the President
PO Box 100
Koror, Republic of Palau 96940
(011)(680) 488-2422
(011)(680) 488-3312

Pennsylvania Emergency Management Agency
2605 Interstate Drive
Harrisburg, PA 17110-9463
(717) 651-2001
(717) 651-2040 FAX
www.pema.state.pa.us/

Puerto Rico Emergency Management Agency
PO Box 966597
San Juan, Puerto Rico 00906-6597
(787) 724-0124
(787) 725-4244 FAX

Rhode Island Emergency Management Agency
645 New London Ave.
Cranston, RI 02920-3003
(401) 946-9996
(401) 944-1891 FAX
www.riema.ri.gov

South Carolina Emergency Management Division
2779 Fish Hatchery Road
West Columbia SC 29172
(803) 737-8500; (803) 737-8570 FAX
www.scemd.org/

South Dakota Division of Emergency Management
118 West Capitol
Pierre, SD 57501
605) 773-3231
(605) 773-3580 FAX
www.state.sd.us/dps/sddem/home.htm

Tennessee Emergency Management Agency
3041 Sidco Drive
Nashville, TN 37204-1502
(615) 741-4332
(615) 242-9635 FAX
www.tnema.org

Texas Division of Emergency Management
5805 N. Lamar
Austin, TX 78752
(512) 424-2138
(512) 424-2444 or 7160 FAX
www.txdps.state.tx.us/dem/

Utah Division of Emergency Services and Homeland Security
1110 State Office Bldg.
PO Box 141710
Salt Lake City, Utah 84114-1710
(801) 538-3400
(801) 538-3770 FAX
www.des.utah.gov

Vermont Emergency Management Agency
Department of Public Safety

Waterbury State Complex
103 S. Main St.
Waterbury, VT 05671-2101
(802) 244-8721
(802) 244-8655 FAX
www.dps.state.vt.us/

Virgin Islands Territorial Emergency Management — VITEMA

2-C Contant, A-Q Bldg.
Virgin Islands 00820
(340) 774-2244
(340) 774-1491

Virginia Department of Emergency Management

10501 Trade Court
Richmond, VA 23236-3713
(804) 897-6502
(804) 897-6506
www.vdem.state.va.us

State of Washington Emergency Management Division

Bldg. 20, M/S: TA-20
Camp Murray, WA 98430-5122
(253) 512-7000
(253) 512-7200 FAX
www.emd.wa.gov/

West Virginia Office of Emergency Services

Bldg. 1, Room EB-80
1900 Kanawha Blvd. East

Charleston, WV 25305-0360
(304) 558-5380
(304) 344-4538 FAX
www.wvdhsem.gov

Wisconsin Emergency Management

2400 Wright St.
PO Box 7865
Madison, WI 53707-7865
(608) 242-3232
(608) 242-3247 FAX
emergencymanagement.wi.gov/

Wyoming Office of Homeland Security

122 W. 25th St.
Cheyenne, WY 82002
(307) 777-4900
(307) 635-6017 FAX
wyohomelandsecurity.state.wy.us

Vital Signs

Temperature • 99.5° F. - 100.1° F.

Red Alert! Although a healthy horse's temperature can vary by as much as 3°F depending on environmental conditions (including stress), a temperature higher than 104°F, and/or cold or patchy sweating is cause for action.

Pulse • 30-40 beats per minute (mature horse)

Red Alert! A pulse rate above 50 bpm (for a mature horse) can indicate distress.

Note that pulse rates vary for younger horses: foals (about 70-120 bpm); yearlings (about 45-60 bpm); 2-year-olds (about 40-50 bpm).

Respiration • 6-20 breaths per minute
(varies widely by size of the horse and weather)

Red Alert! Respiration should never exceed the pulse rate; if it does, get help. More Red Alert signs are short breaths in a resting horse; unusual flare of the nostrils; foam or chewed food in the nostrils; and exaggerated rib-cage movements when breathing.

Capillary Refill Time (CRT) • Less than 2 seconds

Red Alert! If the CRT takes longer than 2 seconds, the horse could be in shock. Also, note the color of the gums or nostril linings: brown, yellow, blue, or dark-red is not normal.

Hydration Pinch Test • Immediate

Red Alert! A fold of pinched skin that does not immediately flatten to normal indicates dehydration. Horses need a minimum of 5 gallons of water daily.

Mucous Membranes • Pale pink

Red Alert! Very pale pink (capillaries contracted indicating possible fever, blood loss, or anemia); bright red (capillaries enlarged indicating shock or toxic reaction); gray or blue (severe shock, depression, or illness); or bright yellow (liver problems)

Intestinal Sounds • Lots of assorted squeaks, gurgles, rumblings

Red Alert! No sounds, or faint, infrequent sounds on both sides.

NORMAL VITAL SIGNS OF MY HORSE

DATE _____

TEMPERATURE_____

PULSE_____

RESPIRATION _____

CAPILLARY REFILL TIME _____

MUCOUS MEMBRANES _____

GUT SOUNDS _____

NORMAL VITAL SIGNS OF MY HORSE

DATE _____

TEMPERATURE _____

PULSE _____

RESPIRATION _____

CAPILLARY REFILL TIME _____

MUCOUS MEMBRANES _____

GUT SOUNDS _____

NORMAL VITAL SIGNS OF MY HORSE

DATE _____

TEMPERATURE _____

PULSE _____

RESPIRATION _____

CAPILLARY REFILL TIME _____

MUCOUS MEMBRANES _____

GUT SOUNDS _____

MY EMERGENCY PLAN

_____

_____

_____

_____

_____

_____

_____

_____

_____

_____

_____

_____

_____

_____

_____

Meet the Author

Ky Evan Mortensen

Author Ky Mortensen has lived and breathed horses his entire life. As a kid growing up on a dairy farm in southern Colorado, Mortensen would often trail ride and camp with his Arabian mare, Bianca. Later, Mortensen rode bulls and played polo at Colorado State University. Having graduated with an equine science degree, Mortensen gravitated toward the Bluegrass State to fulfill his dream of working professionally in the horse world.

After gaining experience working at the Breeders' Cup, The Jockey Club, and the American Association of Equine Practitioners, Mortensen moved from Kentucky to Louisiana to become the director of advancement at the Louisiana State University Equine Health Studies Program. There, he raises funds and awareness for the equine program and handles marketing, public relations, and public outreach.

In 2005, Mortensen — along with members of the LSU Equine Health Team — rescued hundreds of horses following the devastation caused by Hurricane Katrina (and Rita). It was one of the hardest — and most gratifying — times of his life. Mortensen says that *Horses of the Storm* was a story just waiting to be told.

Mortensen lives with his wife and family in Baton Rouge, Louisiana.